STRENGTHS-BASED TEACHING-LEARNING

*A Restorative Approach to
Advance Educational Equity*

Copyright ©2022 by Essie B. Hill, Ed.D. All rights reserved.

Published by Actuate Development Company, LLC
5729 Lebanon Rd, Suite 144229
Frisco, Texas 75034
www.actuatedevelopment.com

No part of this publication may be reproduced, stored in a retrieval system, or transmitted in any form or by any means, electronic, mechanical, photocopying, recording, scanning, or otherwise, except as permitted under Sections 107 or 108 of the 1976 United States Copyright Act, without the prior written permission of the Publisher, except in brief passages included in reviews. The publisher can be contacted at: (phone) 800-992-8571; (fax) 214-387-0299; info@actuatedevelopment.com.

Limit of liability/disclaimer of warranty: This book is intended to provide accurate information with regard to the subject matter covered. However, the author/publisher accepts no responsibility for inaccuracies or omissions, and the author/publisher specifically disclaims any liability, warranty, loss, or risk, whether personal, financial, or otherwise, that is incurred as a consequence, directly or indirectly, of the use and/or application of any of the contents of this book. No warranty may be created or extended by sales or promotional materials. The advice and strategies contained herein may not be suitable for every situation, and this work is sold with the understanding that it does not render professional services. If such services are required, a competent professional should be sought.

The fact that an organization or website is referred to in this work as a citation and/or a potential source of further information does not mean that the author/publisher endorses all of the information that the organization or website may provide. Further, readers should be aware that websites listed in this work may have changed or disappeared between the time this work was written and when it is read.

Bulk orders of this book are available at a discount; please contact the publisher.

Book cover and design: Olivier Darbonville
Author photo: Mohammad Dezfuli

ISBN: 978-1-7320021-3-5 paper back
      978-1-7320021-4-2 e-book

Library of Congress Control Number: 2022903237

Includes bibliographical references.

1. Strengths-based teaching method
2. Public education, secondary
3. Academic Achievement

STRENGTHS-BASED TEACHING-LEARNING

*A Restorative Approach to
Advance Educational Equity*

ESSIE B. HILL

Actuate Development Company
Frisco, Texas

CONTENTS

■

Introduction	**1**
THIS BOOK'S PURPOSE	2
THIS BOOK'S OVERVIEW	6

Chapter 1: Employ Strengths-Based Teaching-Learning: A Method for Building Connections with Students to Improve Learning   **9**

BUILDING POSITIVE TEACHER-STUDENT CONNECTIONS	11
Improving Teacher-Student Connections to Foster a Sense of Belonging	12
Improving Teacher-Student Connections to Build Relational Trust	13
INCORPORATING CULTURALLY RESPONSIVE TEACHING TO DEVELOP RAPPORT AND IMPROVE LEARNING	14
The Potential Benefits of Cultural Competence	17
The Restorative Power of Cultural Humility	19
The Art of Perspective Taking	22
STRATEGIES TO EMPLOY STRENGTHS-BASED TEACHING-LEARNING – A METHOD FOR BUILDING CONNECTIONS WITH STUDENTS TO IMPROVE LEARNING: KEY POINTS	24

Chapter 2: Cultivate Self-Regulated Learning: Supporting Academic Engagement and Performance   **27**

GUIDING STUDENTS TO SELF-REGULATED LEARNING	29
Goal Setting	30
Feedback	31
Reflection	33
EXECUTIVE FUNCTIONS: MECHANISMS OF COGNITIVE CONTROL	37
Strengthening Executive Functioning	38
Executive Functions and Workforce Success	40
METACOGNITION: A MECHANISM TO ENHANCE LEARNING	40
Developing Metacognitive Learners	41
Metacognition and Executive Functions	44
STRATEGIES TO CULTIVATE SELF-REGULATED LEARNING - SUPPORTING ACADEMIC ENGAGEMENT AND PERFORMANCE: KEY POINTS	46

Chapter 3: Tap into Youths' Cognitive Abilities: Using the Multiple Intelligences Approach to Accelerate Learning — 49

MI: A FRAMEWORK FOR UNDERSTANDING COGNITIVE AND METACOGNITIVE ABILITIES — 52
Understanding Executive Functioning from an MI Perspective — 53
Enhancing Working Memory and Cognitive Skills through MI Teaching — 54

ASSESS EXISTING MI STRENGTHS — 56

DEVELOP MI STRENGTHS IN THE CLASSROOM — 58

EVALUATE LEARNING USING AUTHENTIC ASSESSMENTS — 61

STRATEGIES TO TAP INTO YOUTHS' COGNITIVE ABILITIES - USING THE MI APPROACH TO ACCELERATE LEARNING: KEY POINTS — 62

Chapter 4: Foster Resilient Learners: A Framework for Supporting Academic Success — 65

BUILDING HOPE IN THE CLASSROOM — 67
Hope and Goal Attainment — 68
Cultivating Hope — 71

PROMOTING A SENSE OF PURPOSE — 72
Goal Setting — 72
Service-Learning — 73

TEACHING STUDENTS SELF-CONTROL — 75

STRATEGIES TO FOSTER RESILIENT LEARNERS – A FRAMEWORK FOR SUPPORTING ACADEMIC SUCCESS: KEY POINTS — 78

Chapter 5: Collaborate with a Community of Teacher Learners: Making a Strengths-Based Teaching Paradigm Happen — 81

PROFESSIONAL LEARNING COMMUNITIES FOR STRENGTHS-BASED TEACHING-LEARNING — 82

BUILDING COLLABORATION IN TEACHER COMMUNITIES — 86

IMPORTANCE OF RELATIONAL INTELLIGENCE IN IMPROVING COLLABORATION — 87
Establish Trust — 90
Communicate Effectively — 91
Engage in Active Listening — 92
Manage and Resolve Conflict — 93
Employ Perspective Taking and Empathy — 95

STRATEGIES TO COLLABORATE WITH A COMMUNITY OF TEACHER
LEARNERS – MAKING A STRENGTHS-BASED TEACHING PARADIGM
HAPPEN: KEY POINTS   96

Chapter 6: Engage in Continuous Reflection: Bolstering Teachers' Strengths-Based Teaching-Learning Practices — 99

STRATEGIES TO PRACTICE REFLECTION   100

REFLECTIVE PRACTICE AND STRENGTHS-BASED TEACHING-LEARNING   104

STRATEGIES TO ENGAGE IN CONTINUOUS REFLECTION - BOLSTERING
TEACHERS' STRENGTHS-BASED TEACHING LEARNING PRACTICES:
KEY POINTS   106

Conclusion: Strengths-Based Teaching-Learning: Paving an Equitable Way Forward — 109

Endnotes — 113

> **FUNDAMENTALLY, A STUDENT'S STRENGTHS CAN HELP HIM MOVE FORWARD EDUCATIONALLY AND DEVELOPMENTALLY, THEREBY ACCELERATING THE LEARNING PROCESS FOR HIM.**

Introduction

I HAVE HAD OPPORTUNITIES TO WORK IN BOTH UNDERPERFORMING high schools serving mostly low-income students and high-performing schools serving majority higher-income students. The underperforming schools faced the intense challenges intrinsic to high concentrations of students living in poverty. I witnessed a staggering portion of students who had given up. Overwhelming student struggles, chronic disengagement, patterns of poor performance and achievement turned to habits, and ingrained negative mindsets hindered student development and growth to the point of stagnation. A few years ago, I wrote about these experiences in my book *Caring & Engaging Schools: Partnering with Family and Community to Unlock the Potential of High School Students in Poverty*. I had observed how some of the biggest challenges I faced with student performance occurred because of students' loss of hope for the future, disengagement from schooling, and impaired socioemotional wellbeing. As a solution to the challenges, I provided a strengths-based whole child model of public high school that is reinforced by school/family/community partnerships.

During the ongoing coronavirus pandemic crisis, students of all backgrounds are also experiencing hopelessness, disengagement, and impaired socioemotional well-being.[1] Moreover, existing disparities were exacerbated and exposed; now more than ever, we recognize the interconnectedness of all youth as well as that of academic success and social-emotional health. Essentially, pre-pandemic data and patterns inform us of what needs to be done to move forward. We provide our children with strengths-based education, an approach geared toward making conditions favorable for them to thrive both academically and socioemotionally.

Strengths-based approaches have been around for quite some time. They emerged from the field of positive psychology—interestingly, from the application of developments in positive psychology to workplace engagement—as well as from research in education, organizational behavior, and social work. As researchers are continuing to find, a strengths-based education is a more effective teaching approach to improve student achievement than focusing on deficits that teachers need to "fix." Strengths-based educational approaches use strategies to identify what already works well in a child, and more importantly, how each aspect works and can be further developed.[2] It is not about denying that youth have weaknesses and experience challenges or even about neglecting to identify areas for further improvement.[3] Strengths-based instruction, however, does emphasize that the limitations should not be the starting point for increasing student performance because a student's strengths are what empowers him to participate in his learning and development. Fundamentally, a student's strengths can help him move forward educationally and developmentally, thereby accelerating the learning process for him.

THIS BOOK'S PURPOSE

Strengths-Based Teaching-Learning: A Restorative Approach to Advance Educational Equity focuses on practices that contribute to student and teacher success; the challenges both groups experienced during the pandemic crisis invite us to reexamine the way we do schooling. This opportune moment also allows us to reset and grow from adversity, as we reimagine and reinvent education to support all our youth academically and socioemotionally. As we do so, students will be able to visualize themselves in meaningful, purposeful futures. Thus, a viable path forward is to provide a strengths-based education approach to bring equity and excellence to our classroom practices. The practices will empower students to build knowledge, take ownership of their learning, develop skills and awareness, and leverage their strengths to execute and deliver beyond their current states. Students can have strengths in many areas, but the emphasis in this book is on developing students' cognitive or intellectual and socioemotional strengths; these affect how they engage in learning and give them the potential and capacities to develop from who they are right now into who they might become. These strengths are the abilities that will support their academic and social-emotional development.

The purpose of *Strengths-Based Teaching-Learning* is to inform educators about the power of focusing on students' capabilities to motivate and engage them in learning, and more importantly, to offer strategies to apply a strengths-based educational philosophy to their own teaching. Starting with what students can be successful at and building upon cumulative successful experiences will enlist their intrinsic motivation. Though many of the strategies I describe will be familiar, integrating a strengths lens to teaching and learning may be a new concept for many. Adopting an authentic strengths approach would require a paradigm shift in which all educators virtually overhaul their approach to teaching, transforming how they view and interact with their students and provide instruction to them as diverse individuals. Hence, the overarching challenge is for educators to become willing to embrace this way of working with students.

Incorporating this universal intervention will assist teachers in mitigating disrupted learning time caused by the pandemic crisis. School professionals will also be able to support struggling and on-track students—that is, the intervention can be used with a range of different learning needs. Though the legacy of the pandemic is distress and hopelessness, using a strengths instructional lens can counteract feelings of despair by developing and maintaining hope in our students. Hope enables students to move forward—to show up for learning. Research indicates that strengths-based education provides a foundation for building hope in students and fostering their overall well-being.[4] In the process of regaining hope, students begin to discover that they are active agents in improving their own lives—they believe that the future will be better than the present and that they have the power to make it so.[5] The discovery not only enables students to persevere in the face of challenges and adversity, but they are more likely to remain motivated and maintain a positive sense of well-being conducive to academic persistence and overall academic achievement.[6]

It is my hope that this book empowers educators to incorporate the approach in ways that are associated with benefits for student learning and achievement. Strengths-based teaching-learning is a valuable addition to the variety of strategies available to school professionals who want to adopt a restorative approach to promote positive academic and social-emotional outcomes for youth. A restorative approach is a philosophy or guiding principle that sees developing healthy relationships and building community as central to learning, growth, and a healthy school environment.[7] The aim of a restorative approach is closely aligned with the principles of strengths-based education, which include a focus on:

- **Relationship building -** Careful attention is given to establishing authentic teacher-student and teacher-teacher relationships. Teachers who cultivate positive relationships with their students create classroom environments that are more conducive to learning and meet students' developmental, socioemotional, and academic needs.[8] Just as students require caring relationships with their teachers, teachers need supportive relationships with their colleagues, in which they share ideas and solve problems together. In collaborative relationships, teachers often draw support from each other, as they work together to increase student learning and achievement.

- **Whole-child development -** Emphasis is on holistic supports for student development, as schooling goes beyond academic learning. It is also about developing young people's social-emotional skills and involves the development that occurs through relationships, such as those between students and teachers. These whole-child educational practices are primary features of a restorative approach, which recognizes and addresses each student's unique strengths, needs, and interests.[9]

- **Personalized or student-centered learning -** Strengths-based teaching-learning offers a practical method for providing personalized learning instruction; it includes "instructional approaches and academic support strategies that are intended to address the distinct learning needs, interests, aspirations, or cultural backgrounds of individual students."[10] This means that student voice and choice are utilized, enabling students to take charge of and own their own learning—factors requisite for lifelong learning.[11]

- **Equitable education -** In these unprecedented times, it is critical to provide students with strengths-based education; the method will attend to long-standing inequities, offering access to learning opportunities that contribute to a socially just education.[12] An asset-based educational view such as this can uproot inequities, all too common for our most vulnerable children.

This book is primarily meant to support secondary educators in their efforts to educate young people. The strategies can motivate, engage, and support different learners, strengthen and help them to realize high academic achievement, experience positive life outcomes, and reach full potential. Educators will be empowered to awaken transformation, as well as shake off old mindsets and ideologies in order to bring about generational equity for our young people.

THIS BOOK'S OVERVIEW

In the chapters ahead, we will explore six practices or strategies for creating a strengths-based teaching-learning culture to achieve a restorative approach to advance educational equity. The first four chapters cover instructional practices that benefit the whole student, and in the last two chapters, we take a closer look at the practices that build teachers' professional capacity in supporting the philosophy:

Employ Strengths-Based Teaching-Learning: A Method for Building Connections with Students to Improve Learning. Chapter 1 discusses how educators engage in strengths-based teaching-learning practices to build connections with students that improve learning. Teachers do so by cultivating students' sense of belonging and building relational trust. They also incorporate culturally responsive pedagogy, which involves building cultural competence, practicing cultural humility, and engaging in perspective taking skills to improve rapport and embrace learner differences to foster a safe and inclusive learning environment.

Cultivate Self-Regulated Learning: Supporting Academic Engagement and Performance. Chapter 2 explores the importance of cultivating self-regulated learning to support young people's academic engagement and performance. Strategies to guide students to self-regulated learning (teaching students how to learn), include goal setting, feedback, and self-reflection. The chapter also discusses executive functions and metacognition as acutely valuable self-regulatory processes to support student learning; instructional support on both processes can empower students to take effective control of their own learning.

Tap into Youths' Cognitive Abilities: Using the Multiple Intelligences Approach to Accelerate Learning. Chapter 3 focuses on how teachers can tap into students' multiple intelligences (MI) or cognitive strengths to accelerate learning. MI theory is examined as a framework for understanding cognitive and metacognitive skills. We tap into youths' cognitive abilities by assessing their existing MI, developing their abilities through various classroom strategies, and using authentic assessments to evaluate student learning.

Foster Resilient Learners: A Framework for Supporting Academic Success. Chapter 4 provides teachers with a framework or plan to address possible hurdles to academic engagement and learning. Emphasis is on helping students uncover socioemotional strengths by promoting and enhancing the potential for youth to cope effectively with, or adapt to, adversity or other challenging life situations to realize academic and future success. Therefore, we foster resilient learners by building hope in the classroom, promoting a sense of purpose, and teaching students self-control.

Collaborate with a Community of Teacher Learners: Making a Strengths-Based Teaching Paradigm Happen. Chapter 5 shifts to one of the practices that build teachers' professional capacity in making a strengths-based teaching-learning paradigm shift happen. I explore how collaboration in professional learning communities can improve as teachers develop relational intelligence or build better relationships with their colleagues; they establish trust, communicate effectively, engage in active listening, manage and resolve conflict, and employ perspective taking and empathy skills. Educators operate with the understanding that implementing strengths-based instruction to affect change for youth will occur through a team effort.

Engage in Continuous Reflection: Bolstering Teachers' Strengths-Based Teaching-Learning Practices. Chapter 6 also explores a practice that builds teachers' professional ability: engaging in continuous reflection to ensure implementation of high-quality strengths-based instructional practices that foster student growth and development. Educators employ various strategies to practice reflection and participate in both a personal reflection process and critical dialogue or reflections with colleagues.

Reflective practice is further encouraged through the construction of instructional development plans.

The concluding chapter challenges us to use the coronavirus pandemic as an opportunity to recalibrate—to move forward by developing students' academically, socially, and emotionally. It revisits the restorative practices presented in this book; these will help us progress toward educational equity in a manner that attends to whole-student needs. By doing so, we equip students with the tools to fulfill educational potential and life success. We also acknowledge teachers as vital to this process, as they are facilitators of change, helping to lay the foundation for rebuilding stronger an education system that understands the importance of tapping into all students' talents.

CHAPTER 1

Employ Strengths-Based Teaching-Learning: A Method for Building Connections with Students to Improve Learning

STRENGTHS-BASED TEACHING-LEARNING PRACTICES ARE WAYS TO build powerful connections to improve learning and meet students where they are academically—those who are falling behind as well as those who are on track. Students' strengths are positioned as the qualities that build positive connections between teachers and students. This is because the connections help define who students are and who they can become, as well as provide the context in which positive change takes place for students.[1] As a matter of fact, constructive change can occur when we connect young people's strengths and aspirations to curriculum and instruction. We not only affirm students' strengths to help them achieve at their highest capacity but also implement the kinds of learning experiences that can help students realize full potential, while building relationships with them based on the belief that they all have assets that can be mobilized toward academic and socioemotional success.[2]

Teachers operate from the view that students have untapped expertise and knowledge—that is, what students have to say matters in how learning happens. This type of interaction will empower students to be owners of their own learning and reinforce the message that education is ultimately the responsibility of each student in the sense that the student is the one constructing the knowledge and controlling the environment.[3] The more educators give students ownership of their own learning, the greater the likelihood that students are academically motivated and engaged in schooling; they also experience self-worth and a sense of purpose for learning.[4] Hence, engaging students through their strengths is an opportunity to accelerate learning and prepare them for a world in which taking initiative and learning new skills are increasingly paramount to success.[5]

A strengths-based approach emphasizes a relational context that is interdependent; educators engage students as active members in the learning process—in a collaboration that contributes to student success, achievement, and well-being. As partners, teachers and students share experiences, collaborate, discuss what success looks like, and participate in activities that make for engaged learning. In the relationship the teacher becomes a facilitator of learning, recognizing that many of the answers for students' success lie within the students themselves. As facilitator, the teacher provides opportunities that enable students to engage in strategies, relationships, and reflection which involve students' identifying their own strengths, capacities, interests, and goals. This type of safe nurturing relation provides the foundation for each student to begin assessing and implementing a personal value system, as well as gaining an optimistic perspective and a sense of hope for the future.[6]

As educators identify and highlight what already works well in students, and more importantly, how each aspect works and can be further developed (e.g., a young person's intellectual and socioemotional strengths), teachers' bonds with students will be strengthened because of their encouragement and support of each student's best qualities.

Essentially, the bonds will most likely lead to deeper engagement in learning because of the perception that teachers are supportive, caring, and are invested in helping them be successful. Of course, this does not mean that ongoing issues cannot be addressed or that teachers never provide corrective feedback to students. After all, we all have strengths or areas in which we excel and others in which we could use some development. Nevertheless, teachers help youth build from their strengths, while also showing them how to use their strengths to manage areas of weakness or those areas in which they struggle.[7] The support will enable students to commit to personal growth or self-improvement that contributes to incredible results to their academic achievement. Therefore, it is important that teachers learn about their students' strengths and interests, as well as where students are in terms of their knowledge, abilities, and potential.

Building positive connections is one of the most crucial things educators can do to foster student success. The interactions can foster sense of belonging and build relational trust, paving the way for improved connections between teachers and students that enhance learning.

BUILDING POSITIVE TEACHER-STUDENT CONNECTIONS

The most critical function of strengths-based teaching is to build positive teacher-student connections. Connections, teacher-student relationships based on positive interactions and nurturing environments of support and trust, are central to students' willingness to engage in the learning process, their healthy development, and academic performance.[8] In fact, students experience multiple benefits when they have positive interactions with teachers: improved motivation to learn; higher academic engagement, performance, and attendance; elevated levels of social-emotional competence, fewer behavioral problems and suspensions, reduced depressive symptoms, less thoughts about committing suicide, and reduced likelihood that youth will engage in health-compromising behaviors.[9] Moreover, research shows that positive relationships strongly predict whether young people will complete high school successfully, pursue higher education, graduate from college, and achieve economic independence.[10] In essence, positive teacher-student connections are more critical to student success than any instructional strategies teachers provide in subjects such as language arts, math, science, or social studies.

Improving Teacher-Student Connections to Foster a Sense of Belonging

By default, teachers become significant others in their students' lives because they often spend thousands of hours with them in a typical school year. As a result, they become important sources of security and stability for students; generally, a bond begins to develop between teachers and students, creating the foundation upon which a sense of belonging can develop.[11] Belonging refers to a student's belief that he is accepted, respected, included, and supported in the classroom or school social environment.[12] Actually, the psychological sense that one belongs in a classroom and school community is considered a necessary antecedent to successful learning experiences and student well-being. When students feel they belong, they have better academic performance and achievement and are less likely to have mental health problems; students tend to feel optimistic, are more motivated to learn, have higher rates of attendance and expectations of success, and believe in the value of academic work.

Research indicates that higher levels of belonging can lower the risk of academic failure or low achievement.[13] Therefore, teachers who integrate belonging into their practices may offer a way to prevent academic challenges for students. Prevention becomes possible when teachers make connections with young people that make them feel secure and valued—feelings that liberate them to take on intellectual and social challenges and explore new ideas, opening up the opportunity for greater intellectual learning and better outcomes.[14] Generally, teachers avoid deficit language, even when students struggle; instead, they promote an appreciative or strengths-based approach that contributes to feelings of belonging and the enhancement of teacher-student connections.

Improving Teacher-Student Connections to Build Relational Trust

To improve teacher-student connections, educators must take the lead in building relational trust. The trust fostered in the relationship between the teacher and the student sets the foundation for learning,[15] as trust accelerates open communication and an exchange of ideas between the teacher and student. The teacher facilitates the process by establishing psychologically safe, inclusive learning environments where students experience less anxiety, believe it is safe to learn, and feel secure enough to participate.[16] A relationship is established where students believe that educators will provide guidance and instruction that benefit their learning; thus, students feel they can be vulnerable with their teachers, especially when they need help and are struggling. Fundamentally, the trust teachers establish "[provide] the security students need to experience the intellectual discomfort of new ideas and adjust their pre-existing mental models to accommodate new, deep learning."[17] This makes the relationship central to students' willingness to engage in the learning process, academic performance, and their healthy development.[18]

To build a foundation for trusting relationships, teachers take time to communicate what is expected, what is considered successful, and how students will be evaluated. Teachers also commit to listening to and observing students—for example, they find out why students are struggling and then take action to resolve or reduce the problem. By doing so, they create relationships with students that contribute to a trusting learning environment where students believe they are heard, valued, and understood. Good communication such as this builds the connections that make it possible for learning and engagement to take place and for educators to discover students' abilities.

Additionally, relational trust is built when teachers become acquainted with students cultural backgrounds. As they will be working with students from different racial, ethnic, and socioeconomic backgrounds, teachers promote students' unique identities as strengths and assets to school success, and intentionally acknowledge the value of every student's identity.[19] Educators can build trust by creating identity-safe classrooms; in these classrooms, they immediately address put-downs, name-calling, or internalized negative stereotype buy-in to foster prosocial behavior. In this way, teachers ensure that trust does not break down—that their actions and behaviors foster trusting teacher-student interactions. They build trustful relations where students not only believe they matter as individuals in the classroom but are also respected and included in the classroom as well, fulfilling the mandate of an equitable education.

Next, we will focus on culturally responsive teaching as an avenue to develop rapport and improve learning. Culturally responsive practices help teachers create safe, supportive, and inclusive learning environments.

INCORPORATING CULTURALLY RESPONSIVE TEACHING TO DEVELOP RAPPORT AND IMPROVE LEARNING

The rapport between teachers and students is a significant factor in students' learning and success. By incorporating culturally responsive teaching (also known as culturally relevant teaching), teachers can build rapport with students from diverse cultural and ethnic backgrounds. Culturally responsive teaching is a pedagogy that requires teachers to use strategies that connect to students' diverse traditions, drawing especially on the understanding, views, concepts, and ways of knowing students use to maximize their academic achievement.[20] In short, instruction and learning are tied to students' experiences, identities, realities, and histories, and in many ways, their knowledge and expertise. Perhaps, these are some of the reasons a culturally relevant approach to teaching is also viewed as a way to accelerate student learning and improve outcomes for diverse students who are struggling to succeed academically.

Using a culturally responsive approach, educators facilitate how the brain processes information. This means that they draw from students' cultural knowledge by leveraging their brains' memory systems and information processing structures to tap into the way students learn.[21] For instance, when teachers use instruction that includes rhythm, movement, repetition, and visuals, they are using a culturally responsive strategy that is enlarging the neural pathways or cognition of students who learn information best through music and storytelling. In this way, teachers have made learning like students' own cultural learning process. Simply put, culture informs cognition.

Considering our brains are wired to make connections, this strategy makes it easier for students to process, learn, and store information because the knowledge or material is linked to what they already know. As a result, teachers can better prepare scaffolds informed by students' prior knowledge and how they make sense of information, helping them make connections between new concepts and what they already know and making it more likely for neural integration and learning acceleration to occur.[22] Thus, culturally responsive educators empower youth to capitalize on their cultural strengths; they enable students to connect existing knowledge to new concepts and content, while also encouraging academic achievement and socioemotional well-being.[23] Teachers understand that students' experiences are valuable "funds of knowledge" in the teaching-learning process.[24] Thus, they create equitable learning environments for all students when they recognize and use students' cultural components or referents to support learning.[25]

Obviously, educators must get to know or learn about the students they serve. As they learn deeply about the different backgrounds of the students they teach, they begin to recognize that students' cultural backgrounds control how they learn. The understanding allows teachers to choose curriculum and instructional strategies that harmonize with the demographics of the students in the classroom. As a result, teachers present information or themes and content in a way that resonate with unique cultural beings—they make it possible for instruction to be heard by the diverse young people in the classroom. This means that educators should not simply deliver the official curriculum to students but draw from contexts that include students' familial, economic, linguistic, and other aspects of their cultural backgrounds, as well as from situations and experiences to help personalize learning and better meet students' needs.[26] In doing so, educators provide the opportunity for students to find not only personal and cultural resonance, build self-efficacy, and develop higher-level academic skills as they access relevant, engaging, and rigorous curriculum; but they also build bridges to improve connections with their students.[27]

Sometimes, though, personal biases can hinder teachers from truly getting to know their students, ultimately harming relationships and optimal student learning. As a result, culturally responsive educators assess their own personal biases to determine if biases are mirrored in their current practices so they can explore whether unconscious bias might influence their interactions and expectations of students.[28] In doing so, teachers seek to reduce barriers that may cause disparities in student outcomes. This involves thinking about how their own cultures impact their teaching practices. The reflection can help to develop a mindset that strengthens relationships with all students, especially when teachers realize that learning does not happen in the same way for every student, so they provide instruction the way each student learns.[29]

*   *   *

Culturally relevant teaching is grounded in teachers' displaying cultural competence and practicing cultural humility; these qualities will improve teachers' capacity to move toward culturally restorative teaching exchanges and adapt their instruction to fit the needs of a diverse student body. To create ongoing bonds or connections with students, educators can boost their levels in each competency by engaging in perspective taking, as they work toward establishing safe, inclusive, equitable learning environments that foster student success.

The Potential Benefits of Cultural Competence

Cultural diversity is on the rise; consequently, teachers must be prepared to teach a distinct population of students in terms of race, socioeconomic status, language, and ethnicity (diversity increases also include other identifying traits). Now more than ever, the diversity of our children demands that educators—whether teaching in elementary, middle, or high school—become culturally competent. In education, cultural competence is defined as "the ability to successfully teach students who come from cultures other than our own."[30] Culturally competent teachers know about the cultures of the students in their classrooms, as well as about the role culture plays in teaching and learning. They take responsibility for learning about students' cultures and communities so they can use the information as the basis for learning and improving rapport with students. Culturally competent educators honor, respect, and value diversity in theory and in practice, as teaching and learning are made relevant and meaningful to students of various cultures.[31]

Cultural competence enables educators to interact and respond respectfully and knowledgeably with those whose culture and worldview are different than their own. Educators can connect better, though, if they understand their own cultures—their experiences, background, knowledge, beliefs, values, and interests—because these shape their sense of who they are, where they fit into their families, communities, school, and how they interact with students.[32] Nonetheless, connecting with and serving students from diverse cultural backgrounds will enable educators to prevent a cultural gap from impacting students' academic performance and ultimately the achievement gap among different student groups. Thus, culturally competent teachers challenge their own cultural assumptions, values, and beliefs to make a commitment to understand children's experiences, needs, and communication. By doing so, they can also offset stereotypes, promote the development of positive attitudes and behaviors, and build confidence to support learning in all students.[33] In short, the goal is to consider and accept students' differences and backgrounds as strengths or assets, as well as believe that every student can learn.

Although cultural competence enables educators to engage knowledgeably with individuals across cultures, the assumption is that the more knowledge we have about another culture, the more competent we can be in our practices. While it is important in our diverse world to honor cultural differences, the problem is that competency implies mastery and a sense of completion. Educating oneself on others' backgrounds and nationalities still does not give a full picture of the individuals and certainly does not make one an expert in a culture. This is because understanding of a culture is never mastered, especially if that culture differs from our own. Furthermore, the perception of competency limits learning, which is problematic when working with a diverse population. Cultural competence suggests that there is categorical knowledge a person could attain about another group of people, denoting that there is an endpoint to becoming fully competent. This can lead to stereotyping and bias, as cultural competence does not take into account a person's experiences or beliefs that may cause him to have prejudice, biases, or preconceived notions.[34] Why is this information important? These can all lead to low expectations or assumptions about students' capabilities.

However, to establish authentic relationships that lead to positive student outcomes and to help students thrive, educators must go one step further: practice cultural humility. It is the key to success in cultural competence. In essence, cultural competency is a process, not an end product, whereas cultural humility acknowledges we are never done learning about others.[35]

The Restorative Power of Cultural Humility

Cultural humility is a lifelong process of self-reflection, discovery, and self-critique whereby one not only learns about another's culture but starts with an examination of one's own beliefs and cultural identities; it recognizes the shifting nature of intersecting identities and encourages ongoing curiosity. The process also acknowledges and critiques one's own biases in order to build honest and trustworthy relationships.[36] The concept of cultural humility was introduced in 1998 to address inequities in the healthcare field in terms of race, ethnicity, gender, religion, socioeconomic status, geographic location, or other identifying factors. And now the concept is gaining traction in the world of education; practicing cultural humility is deemed to increase the quality of interactions between teachers and their distinct student populations.[37] Similar to being culturally competent, practicing cultural humility can foster inclusivity, empowerment, respect, collaboration, and lifelong learning, as well as counter impediments to education such as stereotyping, marginalization, and stigmatization.

Practicing cultural humility can help teachers examine how their own cultural perspectives affect the way they see students, as their biases and attitudes can affect their relationships with students (see Figure 1-1 for more information on cultural humility and bias). This is especially important, considering the sense of safety and belonging that students feel or have in a classroom or school is directly related to how they perceive bias and stereotypes about aspects of their identities from teachers and others in the school environment.[38] Thus, teachers must constantly acknowledge and reject their own biases, prejudices, and stereotypical attitudes to connect to and honor students' cultures, backgrounds, and experiences to build the rapport that improves student learning.

Although the goal of cultural humility is to understand how culture can inform beliefs, habits, and the choices individuals make, the universality of its principles rejects the false perception that education professionals

FIGURE 1-1

Cultural Humility Requires Historical Awareness

It is not enough to think about one's own values, beliefs, and social position within the context of the present moment. In order to practice true cultural humility, educators must also be aware of and sensitive to historic realities like legacies of racism, discriminatory school discipline practices, implicit bias, tracking by perceived academic ability, and oppression against certain student groups that have led to historic inequities.

To illustrate, culturally relevant teaching shifted from being a strategy of using cultural knowledge to identify what was wrong with children to being an evidence-based teaching strategy to promote teachers use of cultural knowledge for the purpose of improving students' academic performance. Historically, the culture of children of color was positioned as a deficit in comparison to 'mainstream' middle class norms. In turn, the culture of these students was framed as contributing to differences in learning and behavior, thus viewing culture as the key to understanding what was inhibiting the academic success and "positive behavior" of students of color.

The perceived difference between 'mainstream' culture and the culture of different racial groups was described in terms of a gap or deficit that must be fixed. It was assumed that the cultural strategies, behaviors, or pathways typical in middle-class western populations are the normal healthy ones, the benchmark against which children from other cultures should be assessed. Specifically, these unrecognized assumptions about cultural differences influenced teachers' expectations and interpretations of students' academic, social, and emotional behavior. This deficit approach—subtle, but potentially harmful—helps us to understand how culturally based expectations or values have inhibited teachers' positive perceptions and contributed to students' poor performance and even academic failure.

Of course, this belief about youth—and the fact that teachers expected the 'norm'—contributed not only to a history of mistrust and poor relations between white, middle class teachers and students of color but has also led to understandable skepticism about students' feelings of belongingness or inclusiveness in the classroom or school environment. It is worth mentioning here that when individuals/students feel they are not included, they use mental energy to monitor for threats, scan for group barriers, discrimination, and stereotypes; this leaves fewer resources for the higher cognitive processes that should be used for social engagement and learning.

Nonetheless, in order to build trust and improve connections, we first acknowledge and then excavate the historic, systemic reasons for mistrust; we cannot truly heal until we confront the issues and challenges that have contributed to poor relations. This means we must shift from a deficit model of cultural difference to a view that each student brings a unique combination of assets to the classroom and that every student's learning is fostered in an environment that takes those assets into account. It is then that we can build a better future for our children that is founded in practices of cultural humility.

References:

Banks, J.A., & McGee Banks, C.A. (Eds.)(2010). Multicultural Education: Issues and Perspectives, 7th Edition.

Keller, H. (2017). Culture and development: A systematic relationship.

Laldin, M. (2016). The Psychology of Belonging (And Why it Matters).

National Academies of Sciences, Engineering, and Medicine 2018. How People Learn II: Learners, Contexts, and Cultures.

Schmeichel, M. (2012). Good Teaching? An examination of culturally relevant pedagogy as an equity practice.

Sufrin, J. (2019). 3 Things to Know: Cultural Humility.

can become "experts" in the cultures of each of the students they serve.[39] However, the practice of cultural humility does allow educators to understand the complexity of identities—that even in sameness there is difference—and that they will never be fully competent about the evolving and dynamic nature of students' or their experiences. But, they can ask questions to gain a better understanding of their students' cultural histories, experiences, and beliefs. Emphasis is on positive teacher-student connections that involve education professionals examining who they are, what they believe, and why—as well as how these can impact their relationships with students of different cultures.[40]

In a culturally humble relationship, individuals appreciate their own culture while also being open to others; a relationship such as this enables those involved to develop the rapport to work together. To build and heal the teacher-student bond, educators commit to lifelong self-evaluation and self-critique. This means teachers must be humble and flexible, and bold enough to look at themselves critically and desire to learn more, with the understanding that they never arrive at a point where they know all there is to know about young people's cultures.[41] However, educators must listen with interest and curiosity, have an awareness of their own possible biases, and attempt a non-judgmental stance about what they hear and recognize their inherent status of privilege as the facilitator of learning and be willing to be taught by their students.[42]

Educators will be more effective if they are skilled in both cultural competence and cultural humility; utilizing one of these frameworks without the other misses the mark. Nevertheless, educators can improve their levels of competency in each skill by engaging in perspective taking.

The Art of Perspective Taking

Perspective taking will help teachers develop strong bonds with students, as well as help teachers build safe, supportive learning environments.

Perspective taking, a strong factor in culturally relevant instruction, is the teacher's ability to perceive a situation or understand an idea from the student's point of view.[43] As previously discussed, effective instruction depends on teachers' understanding of the complex interplay between learners' prior knowledge, experiences, motivations, interests, language, and cognitive skills; as well as those of educators' own experiences and cultural influences. The complexity and differences, though, often lead to biases, miseducation, and prejudices on the part of school professionals. The good news is that perspective taking has been shown as a means to decrease successfully stereotyping, prejudice, and bias.[44] Research posits that teachers who can take their students' perspectives are more successful in addressing complexities and differences because they take time to learn about and understand the things that affect student learning, including demographics and student strengths, concerns, conflicts, and challenges.

Additionally, a teacher can actively imagine how a student might be perceived or affected by a learning situation; practicing perspective taking in this manner reduces bias and deepens teacher-student relationships.[45] For example, teachers can take their students' viewpoints by learning about and understanding where students come from and where they stand, when preparing for educational learning, forming and/or implementing the curriculum and the instructional material.[46] In doing so, teachers show empathy for students who learn differently.[47] Empathy allows educators to become culturally sensitive to diversity issues, appreciate students' capabilities, as well as develop skills in building and maintaining healthy relationships with students—this includes connecting to, listening to, and engaging students in the learning process.

Teachers' perspective taking abilities and multicultural attitudes enable them to build positive relationships with students and better understand their different learning needs so they can better align their teaching to fit different students' needs.[48] Hence, teachers replace their own frame of reference with the students' perspectives to understand their experiences and the various ways they learn to integrate instruction that engages students in unique and abstract ways, while making the subject content more meaningful and relevant.

STRATEGIES TO EMPLOY STRENGTHS-BASED TEACHING-LEARNING PRACTICES – A METHOD FOR BUILDING CONNECTIONS WITH STUDENTS TO IMPROVE LEARNING: KEY POINTS

Building teacher-student connections is one of the most critical functions of restorative teaching practices. Establishing authentic relationships can be achieved through teaching and learning that is strengths-based; the practices provide the means for uncovering students' abilities and improving learning. In this chapter, we explored these strategies:

- Teachers build relationships with students based on the belief that all students have assets that can be used to enhance their academic and socioemotional lives. The teacher and student enter into an interdependent relationship in which the teacher serves as the facilitator of the learning process; in the interaction, the teacher empowers the student to take ownership of his own learning.

- Educators improve their relationships or connections with young people to promote students' sense of belonging and to build relational trust, setting the foundation for enhanced learning to occur. Teachers provide a curative place where young people can learn in an inclusive and emotionally safe learning environment where they are known, appreciated, and nurtured to develop full potential.

- Teachers develop rapport by incorporating culturally relevant teaching—pedagogy that facilitates and supports the achievement of all students, while requiring teachers to be culturally competent, practice cultural humility, and engage in perspective taking. In this relationship-rich environment, teachers get to know young people as individuals and as learners, which is especially important since teachers and students will need to work together as partners to improve student learning and achievement.

- Culturally responsive teachers acknowledge that racial, socioeconomic, linguistic, ethnic, and other traits create young people's unique cultural makeup—and these enhance their intellectual abilities, not decrease them. In this manner, educators shift from a deficit to an asset or strengths-based mindset to create rigorous student-centered instruction.

> **STUDENTS WHO CAN SELF-REGULATE COGNITION AND EMOTION ARE PRIMED FOR OCCUPATIONAL SUCCESS IN THE 21ST CENTURY.**

CHAPTER 2

Cultivate Self-Regulated Learning: Supporting Academic Engagement and Performance

WHILE BUILDING POSITIVE CONNECTIONS WITH STUDENTS SHOULD be developed because the relationships enable students to take advantage of productive learning opportunities, another complementary strategy of strengths-based teaching-learning should be implemented in parallel: cultivate self-regulated learning to support academic engagement and performance. Self-regulated learning refers to how learners (students) manage their thoughts, feelings, and actions to realize academic achievement. Hence, self-regulated learners are aware of their academic strengths and shortcomings; learners appropriately apply and use diverse strategies to enhance their ability to learn and improve academic performance.[1] The capacity to understand and direct one's own learning is important not only in school but also throughout life. It was during the coronavirus pandemic that we discovered that too many of our young people do not know how to be active agents in their own learning, but the ability to learn independently is especially needed in a fast-changing world. Students who can self-regulate cognition and emotion are primed for occupational success in the 21st century.[2] Thus, self-regulated learning is important to cultivating students' talents or strengths, thereby creating the educational equity that increases access to gainful employment.

The self-regulation of learning spans behavior, motivation, and cognition. Behavior here includes time management strategies, classroom participation, and taking advantage of available resources (assistance from teachers and peers). Motivation (or, affect toward learning) entails awareness and flexibility of beliefs around self-efficacy and goal attainment, in adapting to the demands of academic learning. Cognition involves the command of diverse cognitive strategies (e.g., problem solving, task tracking, and deep, reflective processing strategies essential to learning and performance). Students monitor their behavior within a framework of their goals, reflecting on and adapting their own learning methods to increase effectiveness. Such self-knowledge enhances motivation to continue to improve and likely leads to academic success and more optimistic futures.[3]

To improve students' academic performance, we must commit more time to teaching them how to learn. With the proper instructional conditions and scaffolding, students can gain mastery over the cognitive processes that would help them develop the skills and strategies required to self-regulate better their own learning and to achieve academically. Though it is challenging for students to self-regulate their own learning, they can develop and increase their capacity with instruction and training.[4] Developing students' self-regulated learning skills can make the difference between their academic success or failure. And we must not forget that students play a part in the process as well; they must be willing to invest in learning, curious and willing to explore what they do not know, and apply the skills in order to come to a deeper understanding of academic content.[5] Hence, we will focus specifically on three instructional strategies (goal setting, feedback, and self-reflection) that support teachers in guiding students to self-regulated learning, as well as discuss executive functions and metacognition as self-regulatory tools that support academic engagement and performance.

GUIDING STUDENTS TO SELF-REGULATED LEARNING

In many classrooms teachers assume most of the responsibility for the learning process—a model of learning that many students have begun to depend on. However, teachers can guide students to self-regulated learning through explicit direct instruction, shifting the focus of students' regulation away from teachers to students themselves. By doing so, we enable students to assume responsibility for regulating their own acquisition of knowledge and skills. To make students aware that they are learning how to learn, educators explain to students the usefulness and importance of self-regulated learning skills, as well as support students in identifying when and where they can use the skills or strategies that work best for different contexts or type of learning activity.[6]

It may take time and practice for students to gain effective habits, but instruction on personal, behavioral, and environmental strategies guide students to self-regulated learning, empowering them to engage in learning and improve performance.[7] Personal strategies involve a student's self-efficacy in organizing and transforming information (e.g., outlining, summarizing, highlighting, or mapping); setting educational goals and planning for sequencing, timing, and pacing; keeping records and monitoring through strategies such as note-taking and recording grades; and rehearsing and summarizing through written or verbal efforts to prepare for tests (e.g., use of mnemonic devices, repetition). Behavioral regulation includes self-evaluation and self-observation strategies that occur when a student checks his own progress or work quality. Self-evaluation refers to a student's analysis of the learning task to determine teacher expectations and reflections on what the student desires to accomplish. Self-observation speaks of a student's systematic monitoring of his own performance—verbal or written reporting or quantitative recording of actions to determine progression toward goals. Environmental strategies refer to the use of external sources and creating environments that will optimize learning. These include seeking information from nonsocial sources such as the Internet or the library, seeking assistance from peers and teachers or other adults, as well as ensuring the study environment is in a quiet area so as to minimize distractions, and even dividing study sessions and spreading them over time.

Now we will turn our attention to some common instructional methods that can be incorporated to guide students to self-regulated learning: goal setting, feedback, and student self-reflection.

Goal Setting

Goal setting involves developing, even if implicitly, an action plan or road map to motivate and guide oneself toward the desired end. Self-regulated learners set educational goals; as a matter of fact, the more capable learners believe themselves to be, the higher the goals they set for themselves and the more determined and committed they remain to accomplishing those goals.[8] They direct their cognition to identify the methods for achieving goals, actively pursue those methods, and track progress toward the goals. Learners also monitor activities, thoughts, and emotions to make the necessary adjustments to achieve goals, thereby illustrating commitment to learning and growth. Thus, goal setting enables youth to take ownership of their own learning, supports their motivation and engagement in learning and academic achievement, and makes them more aware of their strengths as well as their limitations.[9] In the process they grow in planning, prioritizing, self-monitoring, and self-direction. These are considered the key 21st century skills needed to become successful in college, workplace, and family life.[10]

In academic settings, personal learning and performance goals are two critically different types of goals that drive students' academic performance and success. Personal learning or mastery goals are behaviors, knowledge, or understandings that a student identifies as important to his own learning. These may include goals related to academic subjects, work habits, learning domains (e.g., knowledge, skills), or a combination of these. By setting personal learning goals, students demonstrate desire to acquire new skills in order to master tasks, and to improve and build learning capacity. Setting personal learning goals produces growth because students actively engage in their own learning—they evaluate class assignment requirements, devise strategies to meet requirements, and monitor their progress to stay on track to goal attainment.[11] Performance goals (challenge- and risk-avoidance goals), by contrast, may demonstrate desire to obtain favorable assessments to avoid negative assessments of competence.[12] That is, the student who sets performance goals may avoid challenging courses because of the belief that "success" is greater when taking easy courses. The student may disengage from goals when confronted with obstacles to success. However, the most effective learners set personal learning goals;[13] students focus on understanding the content, tend to persist in the face of obstacles, and are motivated to take on challenging tasks. Hence, self-regulated learning sees students emerge as fully active participants in their own learning, planning and strategically guiding their behaviors toward achieving self-set learning goals.

Teachers can guide youth to set goals—provide opportunities to practice, not only with regard to content learning goals but with simulated real-life situations that include students' uncovering and satisfying their life passions. And visual tools such as graphic organizers can help students relate more effectively to their progress toward goals, positively reinforcing effort.

Feedback

Feedback is one of the most powerful strategies teachers can employ to influence student achievement; it sends a message to students that teachers care about the learning taking place as well as about their growth and development. Feedback is explanations to students that provide them with insight on how to improve performance or correct mistakes.[14] The explanations should enable learners to understand and monitor their cognitive processes and help them become self-regulated learners who are aware of their most effective strategies for learning, appropriately applying and using strategies independently to enhance their learning and improve academic performance.[15] Students are then empowered to make adjustments in their own learning processes in response to their perception of feedback regarding their current status of learning. To integrate this larger growth process into classroom learning, teachers must provide multiple opportunities for students to use effective feedback—to revise and resubmit work for evaluation against standards. And equally helpful is to tell the learner what he is doing differently than before.

When given correctly, feedback not only guides the student in his learning process but also gives the direction he needs to reach the target or goal of the lesson. In other words, effective feedback requires that a student has a goal, takes action to achieve the goal, and receives goal-related information about how she is doing in her efforts to reach a learning goal. Effective feedback involves a series of actions or steps. Educators provide learners with explanations connected to tangible results related to the goal. The feedback is so transparent that the student is able to learn from it because the descriptions are specific and provide enough information to help the student understand what went well and what did not work, so she can take the necessary steps or actions to improve. Feedback should also be timely (the sooner the better), ongoing (continuous so that the student can adjust performance), and consistent (given useful information that is stable, accurate, and trustworthy).[16]

A discussion of how students can use their talents or strengths to achieve goals should also be incorporated. Formative and summative feedback are involved in this process. Formative feedback that puts progress into perspective should be augmented with summative feedback that emphasizes the strengths and strategies used for recent goal attainment.[17] This includes teachers providing feedback to affirm students' strengths in order to build confidence, as well as emphasizing the strengths students use to approach tasks and providing corrective feedback to call attention to talents or strengths that can be further developed and used to achieve goals. We acknowledge the actions, choices, and responses that lead to goal attainment—specifically, how students process tasks, self-regulate learning, and use their ability to manage emotions and behavior to complete tasks and achieve learning goals. In this manner, feedback boosts students' sense of agency.[18] Hence, potent and timely feedback such as this addresses the development of life strategies grounded in the knowledge of strengths and comments on goal pursuits (refer to Figure 2-1 for a resource on giving feedback to students).

Such evenhanded assistance strengthens students' self-efficacy, and eventually their self-sufficiency as well. Whether critical or encouraging, feedback builds students' belief in their ability to achieve academic and personal goals, both short- and long-term. Constructive feedback such as this supports academic engagement and performance, as students are provided with insights on both areas of improvement and shortfalls, relative to agreed-upon goals or standards—whether knowledge/comprehension, social behavior, performance skills, or learning strategies. The idea is to provide students with the kind of feedback that will increase motivation, build on existing knowledge, and help them reflect on what they have learned.[19]

Feedback is a two-way street; teachers also get feedback from students (see Figure 2-2), especially since they are partners in the learning process.

Reflection

Self-reflection is a self-regulated learning skill students use to assess their progress toward mastery of learning objectives. Consequently, reflection should occur before, during, and after a task. Personal growth

FIGURE 2-1

Giving Feedback to Students

YES	NO	CHECKLIST	COMMENTS AND / OR NOTES FOR IMPROVEMENT
		1. Do you provide information to students making them aware of whether they are on track to achieving the goal(s) of a learning task?	
		2. Do you give descriptive, ongoing feedback related to goals so that students know what and how they need to improve?	
		3. Do you provide feedback in different formats (use of technology, peer-based, one-on-one, verbal, written/ rubrics)?	
		4. Do you present clear, specific feedback so that students understand how the information they are receiving will help them progress toward goal attainment?	
		5. Do you give feedback to affirm students' strengths as well as provide corrective feedback to call attention to talents/ strengths that can be further developed and used to achieve goals?	
		6. Do you ensure students receive timely feedback and opportunities to use it to revise and resubmit work in hopes of better achieving the goal?	
		7. Do you involve students in the process of collecting and analyzing performance data about their own learning, so they are able to recognize their mistakes more easily, helping them to develop strategies and showing them how to use their strengths to tackle areas for improvement?	
		8. Do you acknowledge the actions, choices, and responses students make that lead to their attainment of a learning goal or task?	
		9. Do you provide explanations or insights to students about how they process tasks and self-regulate learning to achieve learning goals?	
		10. Do you suggest options or strategies to help students improve, helping them to stay on track to goal attainment?	

Source: Adapted from Stenger, M. (2014). 5 Research-based tips for providing students with meaningful feedback. Retrieved from https://www.edutopia.org/blog/tips-providing-studentsmeaningful-feedback-marianne-stenger; Wiggins, G. (2012). Seven keys to effective feedback. *Educational Leadership*, 70(1).

FIGURE 2-2
Getting Feedback from Students

How much do you agree or disagree with the following statements?	Strongly Agree	Agree	Disagree	Strongly Disagree
1. I feel challenged in this course/class.				
2. I understand the purpose of the assigned activities or materials in the class.				
3. I understand the content or material that is taught.				
4. I know how to set and pursue learning goals that will help me pass and do well in this class.				
5. When I am given feedback in this class, I know how to improve my performance and correct my mistakes.				
6. I understand the specific goal of a task or learning activity and the criteria by which I should self-assess to determine my progress toward goal attainment.				
7. I receive specific feedback that makes me aware of my areas of strengths or what I do well and areas in which I need to improve my performance.				
8. I understand what is expected on assignments and tests.				
9. I know how to develop strategies to improve my learning performance to reach the learning goals I set.				
10. I receive feedback on how I can use my strengths to monitor and evaluate my own learning to achieve learning goals.				

Identify 2-3 areas of strengths

Identify 2-3 areas for improvement

Source: Adapted from Stenger, M. (2014). 5 Research-based tips for providing students with meaningful feedback. Retrieved from https://www.edutopia.org/blog/tips-providing-studentsmeaningful-feedback-marianne-stenger; Wiggins, G. (2012). Seven keys to effective feedback. *Educational Leadership*, 70(1).

and learning increases when reflection is done before starting a task and when monitoring efforts throughout all aspects of a task, making it more likely to catch mistakes and adjust direction to enable successful task completion.[20] Students account for discrepancies in their understanding and take responsibility for developing an action plan. Afterwards, learners critically analyze their performance in relation to a particular task and consider what they might do differently to improve their performance in future tasks. This involves students reviewing their work and reflecting on their learning progress, enabling them to participate in and take ownership of their own learning.

Self-reflection heightens a student's awareness of his most effective learning strategies and points out areas where he might devote more time and attention. Understandably, effective feedback is an important part of this process. Teacher feedback enables students to reflect on their experiences, allowing them to engage in deep learning and act on feedback to improve academic performance. Jay McTighe provides these open-ended questions to encourage student engagement in self-reflection:[21]

- What aspect of your work do you think was most effective? Why? How so?

- What aspect of your work do you think was least effective? Why? How so?

- What specific action(s) would improve your performance based on the feedback you received?

- What advice would you offer to next year's students to help their performance on this task?

- What did you learn from working on this task—about the content, topic, process, and/or yourself?

To promote student agency, teachers facilitate self-feedback by providing students with opportunities to reflect on their own work; they set aside time for students to analyze where they are in relation to the learning targets. Here are some prompts to help students gather self-feedback so that they get used to owning their own learning:[22]

- What additional questions do I have about this topic?
- What strengths can I identify in my work?
- What aspects of my work am I most proud of?
- How would I improve my work?
- What will I do differently next time?

Students' learning experiences are enhanced, as they can think about why they were or were not successful and then make changes to reach a different or better outcome. In this way, reflection promotes a growth mindset. Both teacher-to-student and student-to-self feedback play an important role in instructing students not just what to learn, but also how they learn and what they can do to improve their learning outcomes. Thus, feedback allows students to reflect critically on their tasks, processes, and learning strategies, as they are afforded the opportunity to identify gaps in their knowledge or skill sets and achieve greater autonomy and deeper learning.[23]

EXECUTIVE FUNCTIONS: MECHANISMS OF COGNITIVE CONTROL

Students can benefit from thinking about the learning process, especially when they can rely on their executive functions to do so—to monitor and control their learning as well as improve their academic outcomes. Executive functioning skills are complementary learning strategies that optimize self-regulation and aid students in their pursuit of goals, allowing them to manage time, plan, focus attention, and handle multiple tasks in order to successfully achieve a goal.[24] Furthermore, youth must rely on executive function skills to obtain knowledge as understanding rather than rote learning, and to participate effectively as actively engaged learners with self-efficacy. Three basic dimensions or primary mental processes are involved: working memory, inhibitory control, and cognitive flexibility. Working memory holds information in the mind while it is manipulated and used in reasoning; it is inevitably at the foundation of executive functioning, as it is where all cognitive operations obtain their information. Working memory enables inhibitory control and cognitive flexibility. Inhibitory control is the self-regulatory skill used to restrain impulses, filter distracting thoughts, resist temptations, pause and think before taking action, maintain focus, and prioritize actions. Cognitive flexibility is the ability to self-monitor—to switch gears and adjust to changes in plans, demands, or viewpoints; to re-establish overall priorities; to change strategies in response to feedback; and to apply skills or rules in their appropriate settings.[25]

Executive functioning may be compared to the air traffic control system at a busy airport. Just as the tower manages multiple planes landing on and taking off from many runways simultaneously to avoid crashes, the well-developed human brain learns to perform complex coordination of ideas, motivations, and priorities.[26] Executive functioning enables youth and adults alike to manage all the streams of information we receive and create, so we can plan projects, see them through, and adjust when situations change. These functions enable students to plan and manage so that they finish schoolwork on time, pay attention to and remember details, evaluate ideas and reflect on their work, and ask for help or seek more information when needed. Clearly, the executive functions directly affect how well students manage school and succeed academically.

Strengthening Executive Functioning

Students are enabled to take effective charge of their own learning with instruction supportive of the executive functions—instruction that should begin in early childhood and continue into the high school years.[27] They will build strengths in several areas: learning capacity, decision making, risk taking, and accountability. The self-efficacy and agency youth thereby acquire can enhance their ability to learn for the rest of their lives, imparting to schooling a lasting impact that both defines and furthers educational equity.

Students will need to have developed executive functioning skills in order to engage in goal-directed or problem solving behaviors; they have to prioritize, organize, delay gratification, follow rules, react to events as they unfold, and cope with frustration. Young people also need developed skills to self-regulate goal attainment; this includes coaching or guidance around planning, persistence, and goal monitoring. Teachers can employ numerous and diverse classroom strategies that provide opportunities to develop executive function skills.[28] Examples include:

- defining specific executive functions and referring to them clearly and frequently as tools for managing one's own learning. Students can be encouraged to share examples from their own lives, in classroom experiences, and in activities beyond school.
- providing opportunities for students to put their executive function skills directly to work. Students can be involved, for example, in articulating learning goals for lessons and choosing topics for classroom projects.
- illustrating effective thinking practices by modeling the "prefrontal cortex"(The prefrontal cortex is the brain region that largely controls executive functions such as self-regulation, self-monitoring, and working memory—functions requisite for focusing on learning). A teacher can explicitly state the purpose for a learning activity and demonstrate the conscious steps involved: planning, implementing, and assessing outcomes.
- recognizing students for using executive function skills effectively. A teacher can observe and indicate not just the strengths and areas for improvement of a completed assignment, but also the thoughtful steps of planning and execution put into its accomplishment.

- providing a well-organized classroom environment with clearly articulated rules to support positive social interactions and productive learning outcomes.

Executive Functions and Workforce Success

The executive functions are necessary not only for academic achievement but also for workforce success. Judy Willis, a board-certified neurologist and middle school teacher who is an authority on classroom strategies derived from brain research, asserts that students can expect to find themselves required by college studies and most job functions to draw upon higher-order attentional and self-regulatory processes.[29] These overall capacities determine the potential to perform at any task that requires judgment, prioritizing, interpretation, critical analysis, self-monitoring, self-correcting, flexibility, resisting immediate gratification to achieve goals, and creative problem solving. Willis also notes that executive functioning undergirds the capacities that employers well into the 21st century will continue to seek, the very skills that artificial intelligence may always lack. The best jobs will increasingly go to those who not only are skilled at analyzing information, but are flexible enough to adapt to revised facts, can collaborate effectively with peers and experts, are willing to consider alternative perspectives, and can articulate and communicate ideas successfully.

METACOGNITION: A MECHANISM TO ENHANCE LEARNING

Metacognition is the process of thinking about one's thinking; it is being aware of and in control of one's own cognitive or mental processes. It is an essential part of teaching and learning and is the "gateway" to students' self-regulated learning behaviors and the main driver of high academic performance.[30] In the metacognitive process, learners use their prior knowledge and experiences to plan a strategy for approaching a learning task; this encompasses selecting, monitoring, managing, and evaluating cognitive processes (mental processes used to construct knowledge or to learn—e.g., memory/remembering, problem-solving, thinking). Learners also self-reflect on how they learn and strategically use the most effective learning strategies to complete their work or achieve a goal.[31] Case in point, when a student is presented with a learning task (e.g., give a presentation on the impact of the COVID-19 pandemic), she has to engage metacognition at every stage of the project, from beginning to end. This means the student has to think through how to approach the learning task, select appropriate strategies, know the purposes these strategies will serve to make a decision about the course of action to use to perform the task successfully, as well as understand how to evaluate use of these strategies in order to monitor her learning and goal progress along the way. However, if the learner does not know how to set goals, plan, and execute the plan, or even know how she learns best to accomplish the task, she will be overwhelmed and very little learning will take place. In short, metacognition is necessary for students to self-regulate their learning effectively.

Developing Metacognitive Learners

Metacognition can be developed in students in the context of their current goals. Developing students' metacognition in this manner contributes to a growth mindset and academic resilience, and enhances students' learning of competencies as well as transfer of learning, no matter their starting point or achievement level.[32] Furthermore, presenting students with consistent opportunities to set and plan short- and long-term, and personally meaningful goals creates learning environments that foster metacognition. To develop metacognitive learners, teachers can utilize metacognitive strategies to help learners guide, regulate, and evaluate their learning. Metacognitive strategies refer to methods used to help students understand the way they learn—strategies in which students "think about their thinking."[33] The strategies help optimize a student's engagement with learning and influence how he interprets the task at hand as well as what strategies are selected and employed in the service of achieving learning goals.[34] With continued practice, students develop the metacognitive skills that equip them to become independent, lifelong learners.

Explicit teaching is one of the most common strategies utilized to integrate metacognitive strategies instruction. What does this involve? Nancy Perry and colleagues suggest that teachers can incorporate these strategies in their practices:[35]

- use explicit language to describe metacognitive processes;
- ask probing questions rather than give answers;
- provide illustrative examples of metacognitive thinking;
- model for students the thinking involved by verbalizing (a.k.a. "thinking aloud") the thought processes used to consider, analyze, and problem solve; and
- prompt students to connect their learning to other topics and experiences.

Additionally, educators develop metacognitive learners by supporting students in the actions they take in order to learn—*planning* (deciding what strategies to use for a learning task and when to use them), *monitoring* (assessing understanding of concepts and effectiveness of learning strategies), and *evaluating* (appraising the plan and adjusting it for future learning).[36] Of course, this support will work better if students have clear learning goals; these are necessary for students to plan strategies that will help them achieve the goals as well as monitor their progress toward goal attainment. Nevertheless, educators can supply learners with the following prompting questions to ask themselves as they engage in learning tasks:[37]

- in the **planning** phase, learners think about the learning goal and how they will approach a task. Learners can ask themselves questions such as these: What am I being asked to do or learn? What prior knowledge will help me with this task? What should I do first? Are there any strategies that I have used before that might be useful? What do I know about this topic?;

- in the **monitoring** stage, learners implement their plan and monitor their progress toward goal attainment. Students may decide to change strategies if the ones they are using are not working. At this time, it may be helpful for learners to ask themselves these questions: How am I doing? Am I on the right track? How should I proceed? Should I try a different strategy? Do I need to try something different?; and

- in the **evaluating** phase, after completing the task, students determine how successful the strategies they used were in helping them achieve the goal. It will help learners to ask themselves these questions to promote evaluation: How well did I do? What did I learn? Did I get the results I expected? What could I have done differently? Is there anything I don't understand—any gaps in my knowledge? Do I need to go back through the task to fill in any gaps in understanding? How might I apply these strategies to other problems?

Scaffolding in this manner guides students to reflect on their learning during activities or tasks, helps them to recognize their strengths and weaknesses, and enables them to plan, monitor, and evaluate their metacognitive thinking better, as well as reuse these behaviors and thought processes on their own when other learning opportunities arise. Essentially, these questions prompt students to engage in internal metacognitive dialogue; they have a conversation with themselves about their learning, the challenges they encounter, and the ways in which they can self-correct to continue learning.[38] How students utilize these skills in the classroom, though, may be dependent on culture and influenced by students' personal characteristics.[39] Nonetheless, students who have the ability to reflect on their learning strategies develop the metacognitive skills that enable academic engagement and performance; they are capable of explaining which strategies they used to solve a problem and why they used the strategies to complete a task.[40] In practical terms, this means students not only know how they learn best, but they also have the capacity to adjust their methods as needed.

By developing metacognitive learners, teachers can potentially create a learning environment where the accountability for education is shared—students are accountable for controlling their learning, and teachers are responsible for guiding, supporting, and facilitating the learning process. Through modeling and coaching, teachers can teach students how to use a range of learning strategies, including the ability to activate background knowledge, plan ahead, and allocate time and memory; to create explanations in order to improve understanding and to note confusion or failures to comprehend; and to evaluate their own work, seek out additional insights, and revise and improve their work. Basically, a metacognitive approach to instruction can help students take control of their own learning, as they would use a set of personalized learning strategies, define their own learning goals, and monitor their progress in achieving them.[41] As students become more skilled at using metacognitive strategies, they gain confidence and become more independent as learners.

Metacognition and Executive Functions

In the metacognitive process learners will need to call upon their executive functions to regulate thinking, as well as manage time, focus attention, plan, and handle multiple tasks to achieve a goal successfully. In short, executive functions play an important role in promoting metacognition in learning; for example, students need inhibitory or impulse control to avoid returning to learning strategies that they metacognitively know will not work based on their past experiences with using them.[42] Moreover, students' executive functioning skills can be strengthened through strategy instruction focusing on helping students become metacognitive learners—by teaching them how to learn. Instruction is most successful when educators include these strategies:[43]

- embed strategy instruction in the curriculum—teach metacognitive strategies (e.g., study skills) linked to classroom assignments or academic content, i.e., how to study for a test;
- explicitly teach metacognitive strategies (refer to the previous section in this chapter); explicit instruction is provided about how, when, where, and why to use them;
- teach strategies in a structured systematic way using scaffolding, modeling, guided practice, and frequent feedback; and
- address students' motivation and self-understanding to ensure generalized use of strategies; students are more likely to use strategies if they are aware that using them will result in improved performance.

Teaching students how to become metacognitive learners is increasingly crucial and valuable to learners of all grade levels, as well as to those in postsecondary education. The process, or how, of learning is consistent at each level and can be modified to address changes in the curriculum as well as the task requirements. As students develop metacognitive skills requisite for effective learning, the competencies enable and encourage students to initiate and persist in tasks, recognize patterns, develop self-efficacy, evaluate their own learning strategies, invest adequate mental effort to succeed, and intentionally transfer knowledge and skills to solve increasingly complex problems.[44] And, they are more likely to develop lifelong ownership of their learning.

STRATEGIES TO CULTIVATE SELF-REGULATED LEARNING - SUPPORTING ACADEMIC ENGAGEMENT AND PERFORMANCE: KEY POINTS

This chapter emphasizes how teachers can support academic engagement and performance when they cultivate self-regulated learning in the classroom. Teachers use these instructional strategies to guide students to self-regulated learning:

- Provide explicit direct instruction on personal, behavioral, and environmental strategies; these not only guide students to self-regulated learning but also enable them to assume responsibility for managing their own acquisition of knowledge and skills. Common instructional practices that influence self-regulated learning include goal setting, feedback, and student self-reflection.

- Guide students to self-regulated learning by developing or strengthening their executive functioning skills. Teachers employ various strategies that include: 1) defining specific executive functions (working memory, inhibitory control, and cognitive flexibility) and referring to them as tools for managing learning; 2) providing opportunities for students to use executive function skills; 3) modeling executive functions such as self-regulation and self-monitoring; 4) recognizing students effective use of functions; and 5) providing a well-organized classroom to support productive learning and social interactions. Students are enabled to participate effectively as actively engaged learners and are equipped to experience success in the workplace.

- Provide explicit teaching on metacognitive strategies to steer students to self-regulated learning. Educators develop metacognitive learners to support students in planning how to approach a learning task, identifying appropriate strategies to complete a task, evaluating use of knowledge and skills or progress, and monitoring comprehension. Instruction enhances students' capacity for self-regulation of learning and increased ability to manage their own motivation, as they are empowered to become independent learners.

> YOUNG PEOPLE'S MI [MULTIPLE INTELLIGENCES] PROVIDE MULTIPLE OPPORTUNITIES FOR THEM TO TAP INTO THEIR INTELLECTUAL ABILITIES, ALLOWING THEM TO LEARN IN A WAY THAT MAKES SENSE TO THEM.

CHAPTER 3

Tap into Youths' Cognitive Abilities: Using the Multiple Intelligences Approach to Accelerate Learning

THE MORE TEACHERS GET TO KNOW EACH OF THEIR STUDENTS THE better they can teach them, in a way that they learn best. Consequently, it is important to extend beyond existing boundaries of cognitive or intellectual strengths traditionally recognized in schools. I suggest starting from the Multiple Intelligences (MI) framework to build on the common recognition that we all best acquire knowledge in different ways. MI approaches are outgrowths of Howard Gardner's assertion that there is much more to being smart than what shows up on traditional intelligence tests, which acknowledge only verbal-linguistic and logical-mathematical skills. Gardner, a psychologist at Harvard University's Graduate School of Education, has long argued that each of us possesses a unique set of intellectual strengths.[1] Gardner developed this view of human intelligence by reviewing case studies of cognitive development—both in normal children and in exceptional cases, such as prodigies and autistic children. He also studied stroke patients and brain-injured individuals who had selectively lost cognitive abilities through acquired neurological damage, providing further evidence to support his view of interacting but distinct intelligences.

Gardner theorized eight intelligences based on the different ways his subjects acquired learning, used memory, performed, and understood subjects: verbal-linguistic, logical-mathematical, visual-spatial, bodily-kinesthetic, musical/rhythmic, interpersonal, intrapersonal, and naturalistic intelligences[2] that speak to youths' diverse and growing cognitive abilities:

- **Verbal-Linguistic** - ability to use syntax, phonology, and semantics of language ("word smart");
- **Logical-Mathematical** - capacity to think conceptually and rationally, and to discern logical or numerical patterns/use numbers effectively ("number/logic smart");
- **Visual-Spatial** - capacity to perceive images and use mental visualization accurately ("picture smart");
- **Bodily-Kinesthetic** - ability to control one's body movements; proprioception ("body smart");
- **Musical/Rhythmic** - ability to perceive and/or express musical forms and patterns ("music smart");
- **Interpersonal** - capacity to detect and respond appropriately to the moods, motivations, and feelings of others; facility in working with others ("people smart");
- **Intrapersonal** - self-knowledge and self-awareness and the ability to be in tune with inner moods, values, beliefs, thinking processes, and motivation ("self smart"); and
- **Naturalistic** - ability to draw distinction about the natural world—recognizing and categorizing plants, animals, and other objects in nature ("nature smart").

Once we recognize and even embrace that individuals have varied kinds of intellectual strengths, then education that treats everybody uniformly is seen to be the most unfair way to teach.[3] Far more effective is to help all students understand and develop their cognitive strengths, while guiding them to become responsible for their own knowledge acquisition.

The MI approach is a flexible pedagogy that emphasizes student voice and choice; consequently, teachers can take cultural factors into consideration with its implementation, helping to ensure schooling is equitable for all students. Student voice describes how students give input to what happens in the school and classroom; this involves instructional approaches and techniques based on student choice, preferences, perspectives, passions, and ambitions.[4] By applying MI in the classroom, teachers adapt instruction to give students a voice in how they learn; teachers take into consideration the different ways students learn best and reinforce students' intelligences by including learning experiences that resonate with how each student processes information. This ultimately allows for a student-centered process that will enable each learner to use his specific abilities to engage in and demonstrate learning. In fact, motivation will improve for many disempowered students—historically marginalized populations, including students from Black, Latinx, Native American, and low-income communities as well as students with disabilities—who struggle to succeed with traditional learning and teaching methods (those where we expect every student to learn in the same way and at the same time).[5] However, when teachers acknowledge their diverse multiple intelligences and needs and facilitate student voice, they can observe how students express themselves and demonstrate their growth and learning around content standards via modalities that draw upon their natural strengths. Such knowledge is invaluable in informing change and to the teacher designing instruction to meet individual student needs.

Student choice is considered one of the best strategies a teacher can use in the classroom to engage students.[6] Giving students choice means providing them with options and allowing them to choose what works best for them. Young people's MI provide multiple opportunities for them to tap into their intellectual abilities, allowing them to learn in a way that makes sense to them. Then, it is not surprising that the options MI theory provide students with positively impact their learning and engagement, contribute to enhanced motivation, interest, and commitment to academic tasks in a manner that accelerates learning. This is because the MI model provides at least eight potential pathways to facilitate effective learning and opportunities to engage students' strengths, interests, and goals for learning.

MI: A FRAMEWORK FOR UNDERSTANDING COGNITIVE AND METACOGNTIVE ABILITIES

MI is a theory of cognitive functioning that proposes everyone possesses significant and usable amounts of each of the intelligences, and they function together in ways that are unique to each individual.[7] Some profiles display fairly equal balances of several intelligences, whereas in others one or two intelligences predominate. Nonetheless, individuals can use their cognitive abilities to process information and express meaning, as well as convey understanding in different ways, unless compromised by severe congenital/ developmental defects.[8]

Applying the theory in the classroom enables teachers to use students' MI strengths to accelerate learning, as MI can assist learners in the developmental use of metacognitive skills; learners' metacognitive skills will also help guide them in their acquisition of knowledge or the ability to learn new information. This means that MI provides learning capabilities that can lead to the development and use of metacognitive skills that students utilize to manage their own learning—for example, on tasks such as student projects of choice. In any academic discipline, educators can use the theory to teach students the skills of managing their own learning by giving specific guidelines to conduct projects.[9] Guidelines may include having a student identify the goal of her project and the sources of information that will be used, describe the steps to achieve the goal, list possible methods for project presentation (e.g., constructing models), organize the project into a timeline, and decide how to evaluate the project. Through this explicit instruction, students not only naturally engage several intelligences by working through these guidelines, but they also gain academic self-efficacy by employing these metacognitive learning strategies. Thus, students are enabled to believe they will be successful in project completion and capable of achieving academic success.

Understanding Executive Functioning from an MI Perspective

Seana Moran and Howard Gardner have suggested that the executive functions are vitally powered by intrapersonal intelligence, the cognitive ability that processes information relevant to and about the self.[10] Intrapersonal intelligence analyzes information pertaining to abilities, emotions, aspirations, beliefs, sensations, and self-presentation, enabling self-understanding and awareness. Moreover, it modulates all aspects of the self by recruiting executive function skills. In a sense, then, the executive functions direct the other intelligences toward purposes pertinent to one's self—such as the self-regulated learning behaviors that sustain a student's motivation to achieve educational aspirations and realize visions of the future.

If intrapersonal intelligence maintains the map that organizes the self, then executive functioning is the compass that indicates direction along the roads for developing, expressing, or enhancing the self. To gauge map instructions, as Moran and Gardner propose, the executive functions integrate three factors: "hill, skill, and will." The hill is the best possible self—the aspiration that inspires efforts to become who the individual wants to be. Skill is the abilities and techniques for attaining goals, drawing upon any or all intelligences. Will generates the ongoing effort and motivation to persevere until goals are reached.

Furthermore, confidence is empowered when students successfully recruit their particular abilities to achieve favorable learning outcomes.

They consequently develop higher self-efficacy and extend their aspirations through being recognized and valued—by adults and by their own selves—for who they are and how they best learn. Youth learn to self-regulate, ultimately, through growth in self-knowledge of their individual MI profiles.

From the MI perspective, therefore, self-regulated learning is not a fixed skill: As students' strengths continue to develop consciously, they discover further means to parlay cognitive growth into favorable performance. In particular, while dominant intelligences are favored in processing academic content, less favored intelligences can develop and grow through leveraging of existing strengths. MI theory therefore yields more than alternative approaches for keeping younger students entertained; it also produces pathways for teaching increasingly rigorous knowledge and skills to older students as they learn to use their brains more effectively and fully, self-regulating their learning across varied contexts.

Enhancing Working Memory and Cognitive Skills Through MI Teaching

Working memory (WM) has a significant impact on how well students can possibly perform in school and beyond, as do their broader memory skills. In daily life we use WM as a fundamental tool to accomplish cognitive tasks—from following through with elaborate plans, to deciding what we should do next when circumstances change. Working memory holds onto new information while we make sense of it, focus and refocus our attention, and manipulate our perceptions and our verbalizations (using "cognitive flexibility"), over the short periods of time needed to complete cognitive tasks. In any demanding or enriched environment, WM also enables "inhibitory control," used to resist distractions and irrelevant information.[11]

But is an MI approach not only reassuring and validating, but also efficacious? Research indicates that learning through multiple modalities is an effective way to boost memory and understanding. To illustrate, students can retain more information when instruction is complemented with diagrams, illustrations or images.[12] This means that when students are processing lesson content through more than one medium, learning is more deeply encoded. Thus, when we give students multiple ways to process information, the lesson will be more engaging and students are more likely to remember information that is presented in different ways.[13]

Consider the relationship between WM (the all-purpose executive function), and higher-order processes (critical thinking and problem solving). These two cognitive skillsets, both vital to academic learning, routinely interrelate: WM facilitates higher-order thinking, as when we reason we draw repeatedly upon what is temporarily stored in working memory. And "memory," the retention and retrieval of knowledge, includes far more than recalling information: Higher-order thinking is called upon to apply newly encountered ideas, which must be held in and made available by WM. Using critical thinking, we reason through and decide what to believe or what to do; as problem solvers, we deduce a path or solution to reach a goal. Higher-order processes thus enable students to evaluate, analyze, and synthesize information—to create knowledge, empowering youth to be creative and innovative, to develop multiple viewpoints, to use good judgment, and to make sound decisions—that is, to become adults. However, to accomplish any of this, students must be able to hold and use information in working memory.

The MI framework, fortunately, inspires methods for reaching all students, enabling opportunities for higher-order thinking to be implemented effectively across the curriculum. In an intriguing point, Gardner posits that all forms of memory are specific to particular intelligences.[14] Thomas Armstrong extends this idea to a practical argument in *Multiple Intelligences in the Classroom*.[15] Some students might have an excellent memory for faces—an aspect of visual-spatial intelligence—but struggle with names and dates, i.e., with the verbal-linguistic and logical-mathematical intelligences given primacy by conventional educational methods. Many such children, along with so many other sorts, become assessed as weak in higher-order thinking and wind up self-identifying that way as well. But if helped in school to gain access to and develop memory skills through other intelligences, they might instead blossom as learners.

This point is particularly important for students with impaired working memory (e.g., students with learning disabilities, students living in poverty—due to toxic stress). Armstrong contends that schoolwork involving recall skills (which trains both long-term and working memory) should be conducted such that several types of memory are activated. That is, teachers should differentiate and/or enrich instruction to associate the material with components spanning intelligences (e.g., words, numbers, pictures, musical phrases, gestures). Exposure to learning that draws upon memory associated with all eight intelligences enables students to orient toward and focus on those that work best for them, providing them with self-assimilated study skills and learning tools for effectively internalizing and applying ideas.

ASSESS EXISTING MI STRENGTHS

The MI framework strives to help students identify and build from their existing cognitive skills. Such success, however, depends on the educator's commitment to discovering which modalities best connect with students' strengths and favored intelligences, plus developed skills in modifying instruction to fit needs as well as assets. As a result, students are more likely to engage in the learning opportunities offered to them. In an effort to maximize students' interest in academic subject matter and their own learning proclivities, educators will first need to teach their students a bit about MI. By doing so, educators broaden students' understanding that they are all intelligent or smart in different ways. When students learn what their innate capabilities are, they can determine the most effective way for them to learn (i.e., learning can take place through their most highly developed intelligences). Thus, teaching students about the multiple intelligences theory shows them they each have something important to offer in every class or situation, and that their differences are strengthens to fulfill potential. Instruction about each of the eight intelligences can be brief but definitely depends in part on class size, the developmental level and background of students, and the instructional resources available.[16]

After explaining the theory to students, follow up with a self-assessment for each student. This allows educators to identify accurately what students strengths are; students will be able to capitalize on their strengths and work on developing their weaker ones. However, the best tool for assessing students' existing strengths is probably observation; observing how young people approach problems and make products reveals much about their intelligences.[17] These are diagnostic indicators of how students learn most effectively. Hence, assessment of strengths will not only give educators a snapshot of students' innate abilities, but the results from the assessment will also provide a springboard of strengths from which teachers can engage in positive relationships with students, whether on a semester or year-long basis.[18]

Through innovative MI-inspired assessments, young people can come to better understand how their minds learn. One such assessment is the rigorous and validated Multiple Intelligences Development Assessment Scales (MIDAS™); it is an assessment tool created by Branton Shearer to enable all students to identify their intellectual strength profiles through a twenty-minute questionnaire. According to Shearer, the MIDAS™ provides parents and teachers a depth of perspective on intellectual style, activities, and tendencies not available from other such aptitude tests.[19] Howard Gardner argues, however, that feedback and insights from students themselves must be corroborated by input from parents and teachers, to validate and support self-reported or even self-assessed strengths and weaknesses.[20] The importance of drawing others into the discussion about student strengths, rather than relying solely on self-report, is that often people will recognize characteristics, capacities, and resources that individuals do not realize about themselves. It can also be useful to have these discussions at various points through the school year as development, changes, and new experiences can be noted and reflected upon as the strengths picture develops.

Self-assessment of strengths helps students learn more about their intellectual identities and can further develop self-awareness. Students' exploration of strengths through various assessments facilitates self-exploration that help students discover their strengths and capacities and can orient students to appropriately direct their motivations and behaviors toward academic goals. A MI assessment is also valuable in determining an individual's potential to solve problems or fashion products that can be of use to society.[21] Young people's assessment results will help them begin to develop vocational aspirations. Once students know and understand their multiple intelligences, they become more aware of well-suited career options they might pursue, as they are pointed in the direction of potential career areas and disciplines to explore for which their particular intelligences may apply. For example, a student who excels at the interpersonal intelligence may explore counseling or psychology, or a student whose dominant intelligence is logical-mathematical may explore STEM careers. That is, measuring students' natural talents can assist them in developing the critical thinking skills that help them become aware of occupational roles that align to the adults they might be in the process of becoming, allowing them to contribute to a more productive workforce and citizenry pipeline.

DEVELOP MI STRENGTHS IN THE CLASSROOM

Merely identifying and affirming strengths may inadvertently encourage students to adopt a fixed mindset, but educators should use developmental interventions, recognizing that strengths are not static traits but are dynamic qualities that can be developed over time.[22] Enabling students to acquire a deeper understanding of their individual strengths and a sense of their evolving intellectual identity, teachers diagnose how best to help develop each student, based upon their MI strengths or cognitive abilities, as well as not-yet-realized intelligences and talents. The information can inform instruction and be used as a springboard to discuss potential, goals, and challenges; discussions with students should involve how to utilize their strengths in ways that will be of value to their academic success, i.e., using strengths to master course content.

With proper encouragement, enrichment, and instruction, most developing individuals have the ability to develop all eight intelligences to a reasonably high proficiency level. Critical to emphasize here, though, is that a student's preferred mode of learning ought not to dictate exclusive focus upon that domain, at the expense of developing others.[23] Youths must learn to function by drawing upon several of their intelligences, all of which can and should continue to develop over a lifetime. Similarly, underdeveloped or disfavored intelligences ought not to be used as an excuse for students to underperform in or neglect certain subjects; on the contrary, each student should learn to leverage intelligence strengths and preferences across domains. The objective, however, is to aid students in applying their strengths in the learning process, in intellectual development, and in academic achievement so that they can reach previously unattained levels of personal excellence.[24]

In a teacher training document entitled "Different Kinds of Smart: Multiple Intelligences," Linda Darling-Hammond and colleges, with contributions from Howard Gardner, review ways to develop all eight intelligences in the classroom. The document identifies three dimensions of classroom application of MI theory: 1) assessing and building on students' strengths, 2) providing multiple entry points to content, and 3) creating interdisciplinary curricula.[25] Assessing and building on students' strengths helps teachers understand students as self-sufficient learners who also need opportunities to strengthen their abilities and self-confidence in particular modalities. By providing multiple points of entry as they introduce new subject matter, teachers empower students to gain different perspectives on the same topic, while also deepening their understanding so they can go beyond rote recall to finding new ways to represent and apply what they have learned. Interdisciplinary curricula, in turn, require students to practice and apply diverse skills they have cultivated across topics and learning approaches, strengthening all students' intelligence profiles while increasing retention through making content more meaningful.

Thomas Armstrong points out that though the MI model provides at least eight potential pathways to facilitate effective learning, teachers need not attempt to teach every topic in eight different ways.[26] Teachers can, however, provide a reasonable variety of intelligence-based options—whichever are most relevant or effective for each concept—so that students can build skills in deciding which pathways interest and suit them most. This also involves carefully selecting activities that not only teach to the intelligences, but also realistically mesh with the subject matter of the lesson or unit. Meanwhile, Armstrong offers a seven-step procedure for creating a classroom curriculum that comprises varied lesson plans reflecting the MI approach:

- focus on each specific objective or topic;
- pose questions raised by MI theory;
- brainstorm or research possible strategies for each intelligence;
- consider a range of techniques and materials;
- select promising activities;
- set up a sequential plan around an appropriate series of objectives or topics; and
- implement the plan with a mind open to responsive change.

In their research-grounded practical guidebook, Mindy Kornhaber, Ed Fierros, and Shirley Veenema identified what they call "compass points"—practices directed toward engaging students' MI in ways associated with student learning.[27] These systemic practices emphasize several factors. Hardworking teachers care about educating diverse learners and believe in and respect students' strengths and potentialities. The most supportive instructors are also committed to accessing varied avenues for learning and demonstrating knowledge; they view the multiple intelligences as integral, not peripheral, to cultivating skills and talents, enabling all students to tackle the breadth of the curriculum. Through formal and informal exchanges of ideas, collaborative educators should share constructive suggestions, drawing on the knowledge and strengths of their colleagues to complement their own areas of strength.

EVALUATE LEARNING USING AUTHENTIC ASSESSMENTS

MI theory proposes a fundamental restructuring of the way in which educators assess their students' learning progress. It suggests a methodology that relies far less on standardized or other formal types of tests (normative or traditional assessment) but involves students themselves as an integral part of the assessment process (student voice).[28] The MI philosophy of assessment is closely aligned with authentic measures of assessment that probe students' understanding of material far more thoroughly than do short answers to specific questions, multiple choice, or even fill-in-the-blank tests.[29] These assessments or meaningful expressions of students' learning process should demonstrate their higher-order thinking skills and should be carried out in the context of units or projects to tap into several intelligences;[30] students can show what they have learned in their classes through presentations, portfolios, videos, observations, recorded anecdotes, and more. By doing so, teachers can track MI growth and development over time.

The educator provides multiple options for how student learning can be demonstrated and assessed, allowing students to select the project or assessment type that most closely resonates with their own particular constellation of strengths.[31] Building these choices into assessments gives students an element of control. Rather than trying to keep assessments the same whether students are learning face-to-face, in a hybrid environment, or remote, building choice into assessments has the potential to create greater levels of student motivation and engagement.[32] As research notes, students are more engaged and learn best when they are given various ways to demonstrate their knowledge and skills; this also helps teachers to assess student learning more accurately.[33]

The theory supports the belief that students should be able to show competence in a specific skill, topic, content area, or domain in any variety of ways. And just as the theory of MI suggests that any instructional objective can be taught in at least eight different ways, it also supports the idea that any subject can be assessed in at least eight different ways. The idea is to provide students with authentic assessment experiences that include access to a variety of methods of presentation (inputs) and means of expression (outputs). The types of assessment experiences that MI proposes—particularly those that are project-based and thematically oriented—offer students frequent opportunities to be exposed to several of these contexts at one time.[34]

STRATEGIES TO TAP INTO YOUTHS' COGNITIVE ABILITIES - USING THE MI APPROACH TO ACCELERATE LEARNING: KEY POINTS

Teachers are enabled to tap into the intellectual strengths of each student and further draw out and nurture intelligences in each student when they implement the MI approach to accelerate learning. They draw students back into learning, as they will use different intelligences to teach a concept, thereby giving students greater chances to succeed at learning. The MI framework inspires methods for reaching all students, as the theory states that everyone has all eight intelligences at varying degrees of proficiency. This chapter focused on these tactics:

- Draw on students' cognitive abilities by using MI theory as a tool for understanding executive functions and enhancing working memory and cognitive skills through MI teaching. This includes providing instruction to help all students understand how their cognitive abilities or intelligences enhance their metacognitive strategies, ultimately helping them to become responsible for their own learning.

- Assess students' existing MI strengths, enabling them to engage in a self-discovery process where they uncover the answers to vital questions such as "How do I learn best?" or "What are my unique innate strengths?" Measuring students' intelligences allow educators to facilitate development of students' natural talents to support their cognitive growth.

- Utilize various classroom strategies to facilitate development of students' MI strengths: 1) assess and build on students' strengths, provide multiple entry points to content, and create lesson plans that reflect the MI approach; 2) provide a reasonable variety of intelligence-based choices to mesh with the subject matter, lesson, or unit, in addition to creating lesson plans that reflect the MI approach; and 3) access different avenues to support student learning and demonstration of knowledge as well as draw on the knowledge and strengths of colleagues to adopt a MI approach.

- Use authentic assessments to evaluate student learning. Allow students to show what they have learned through presentations, portfolios, videos, observations and recorded anecdotes; to name a few. These should be meaningful expressions that demonstrate higher order thinking skills.

> SCHOOLS MUST SEEK TO ADDRESS STUDENTS' SOCIOEMOTIONAL WELL-BEING, AS IT IS VITAL FOR OUR CHILDREN TO ACHIEVE ACADEMIC, WORK, AND LIFE SUCCESS.

CHAPTER 4

Foster Resilient Learners: A Framework for Supporting Academic Learning

STRENGTHS-BASED INSTRUCTION NOT ONLY TAKES INTO consideration student learning but also student struggles; the method will help students with the nonacademic issues that critically interfere with optimal learning and life success. As any study of learning clearly shows, well-being and learning are interconnected. In reality, academic performance itself depends on students' health in mind, body, and spirit. Healthy students feel safe, content, and connected to purpose, people, and community, as well as peaceful, energized, and resilient. Consequently, we want to create educational conditions that foster resilient learners—those who succeed in school despite the presence of adverse conditions or personal challenges.[1]

As concerned educators and other stakeholders nurturing the next cohort of adults, we have a responsibility to cultivate the holistic well-being of our young people, too many of whom struggle profoundly in today's overwhelming society. Consider the fact that American students were experiencing widespread mental health issues long before the COVID-19 pandemic crisis. Findings indicate that youth experience chronic stress and mental health challenges associated with adverse childhood experiences that cause trauma (e.g., abuse), as well as struggles with anxiety, depression, suicidal ideation, and suicide.[2] Nearly two years into the pandemic crisis, depression and anxiety have doubled in children and adolescents; suicidal ideation rose among children and young adults, in addition to a striking rise in youth suicide.[3] Thus, we want to support youth by actively teaching them not just to survive, but to be resilient in the face of adversity. These challenges cannot and must not be denied; moreover, we do not overlook the fact that young people will experience the emotional pain that comes with adversity or trauma. But we want to equip youth to reduce the likelihood of creating a dependency that is disempowering, resulting in recurrence as patterns. By teaching students to be resilient, we help them develop the socioemotional strengths that allow them to tackle problems on the way to recovery and view the circumstances as opportunities for change and growth.

Tackling adversity via strengths reveals that every person holds the key to her own particular transformation through meaningful development. Strengths-based approaches are process-oriented, using distinct language of change and growth to describe students' struggles. Education that emphasizes strengths, capabilities, and resources empower a youth to see opportunities and solutions rather than just a restricted vision of his current problems and hopelessness.[4] Therefore, students use strengths as the starting point for building resilience.

A strengths-based approach is grounded in the assertion that all students have emotional and behavioral strengths and capabilities that they can learn to leverage to buffer against developing mental health problems, or at least to mitigate their severity.[5] Emotional strengths may include such internal coping abilities as facing and rebounding from challenges or reframing setbacks as opportunities. Behavioral strengths may include self-management skills, social skills such as assertiveness and accommodation, effective goal setting, or sound decision-making. Ultimately, understanding their own socioemotional strengths can help all students reduce stress and maintain hope in the face of adverse life circumstances.[6] Thus, building students' socioemotional competence is implicit in fostering resilient learners. With this in mind, we focus on building hope in the classroom, promoting a sense of purpose, and cultivating self-control in students. By doing so, we enable students to engage or reengage in learning, as well as nurture their capabilities in personal discipline and work habits necessary for improving and achieving positive academic outcomes. This valuable support will help young people while they adjust in the face of personal, family, school, and community adversity so that they do better than expected in school, given the risk status.[7] In the cause of educational equity, schools must seek to address students' socioemotional well-being, as it is vital for our children to achieve academic, work, and life success.

BUILDING HOPE IN THE CLASSROOM

Hope matters, especially in a time of uncertainty and in the struggle for equitable education, as loss of hope dramatically affects students' motivation to engage, belief that they can set and achieve goals, and attitude that they can learn, develop competencies, and eventually succeed. Loss of hope is a primary indicator of disconnection from school; disengagement and hampered well-being both spring forth from hopelessness and yet have distinct origins and features of their own. Unfortunately, youth who believe more broadly that they have a promising future, nevertheless, also lack hope that effort and success in school can help them get there. But students need to see themselves conquering obstacles, problems, and setbacks to feel convinced to participate actively in the learning process. Hence, we build hope in the classroom even when nothing is normal, as hope serves as an anchor for the mind. This anchor enables stability and confidence, helps students to hold on and be encouraged, and empowers them to move forward educationally and developmentally.

Hope is belief that the future can be better, whether in school or in the rest of life; it is not an emotional state, a tendency toward positive or wishful thinking, or a naive optimism. Being hopeful, however, makes us better able to take action and transform ourselves in the present by believing the future can improve as a result of our actions. That is, hopeful individuals discover that they have agency in working toward that brighter future; they tend to persist and not give up. Research shows that when our children have hope, they have a tendency to perform better. For example, Shane Lopez, author of *Making Hope Happen: Create the Future You Want for Yourself and Others*, found that a hopeful student is 12% more productive and achieves up to a letter grade higher than a less hopeful student of equal intelligence.[8] In fact, hope is a cognitive outlook that predicts future academic achievement more specifically than do measured intelligence, stable personality traits, or even previous academic achievement.[9] It is the foundational antecedent to academic success and the psychological vehicle that drives the nonacademic, or at least highly emotional, factors—well-being, resilience, willingness, goal setting, managing obstacles, and determination—that impact academic achievement. Thus, addressing this social and emotional aspect of growth and learning will empower youth to engage in learning, achieve academically, stay in school and graduate, and be successful in college or other postsecondary education.

Hope and Goal Attainment

We build students' hope and hopeful thinking to get them to buy into their futures. This is because hopeful individuals are motivated to conceptualize goals (goal setting), develop strategies to reach those goals (pathways), and initiate and sustain the application of those strategies (agency).[10] All three are action-oriented components necessary for supporting goal attainment, which is the essential attribute of hope as a character strength (see Figure 4-1 for an activity that can be used to guide goal setting instruction). Hope provides the belief, will, and determination to work to attain goals, as well as the resilience and

FIGURE 4-1

Hope Activity

1 - Always like me   2 - Mostly like me   3 - Somewhat like me   4 - Rarely like me   5 – Not at all like me

Goal Setting – hopeful individuals are motivated to conceptualize goals (what they hope to accomplish in the future, whether short-, mid-, or long-term)

- [ ] 1. I set clear and specific goals (e.g., personal, academic).
- [ ] 2. I set several goals so that when I face a profound blockage in one goal, I can turn to my other important goals.
- [ ] 3. I rank my goals by their importance.
- [ ] 4. I set clear markers for goals (e.g., "to study an hour each day in preparation for my next science test").
- [ ] 5. I establish goals that yield a large return.
- [ ] 6. I establish "we" goals in addition to my own "me" goals.

Pathways – set of different strategies to reach goals

- [ ] 1. I break down long-term or large goals into smaller steps or subgoals.
- [ ] 2. I spend time thinking about what I need to do to accomplish my goals; this includes identifying several routes to achieving my goals.
- [ ] 3. I try other routes or strategies if one pathway does not work.
- [ ] 4. I do not attribute a blockage to my lack of talent but search productively for another route that may work.
- [ ] 5. If needed, I learn new skills to reach my goals.
- [ ] 6. I ask for help when I need it.

Agency – motivation to pursue goals and persist toward goal attainment

- [ ] 1. I make goals based on my internal, personal standards, not those imposed by my peers, parents, or teachers.
- [ ] 2. I set "stretch" goals based on my previous performances.
- [ ] 3. I engage in positive self-talk to encourage myself toward goal attainment (e.g., "I can do this."; "I will keep at it.")
- [ ] 4. I encourage myself by recalling my previous successful goal pursuits and reading stories or other resources that depict how other students have overcome adversity or have succeeded.
- [ ] 5. I learn to enjoy the process of getting to my goals and do not focus only on the final attainment.
- [ ] 6. I find a substitute goal when the original goal is blocked solidly.

Source: Adapted from Lopez, S. J., Rose, S., Robinson, C., Marques, S. C., and Pais-Ribeiro, J. (2014). Measuring and promoting hope in schoolchildren. In M. J. Furlong, R. Gilman, and E. S. Huebner (Eds.), *Handbook of Positive Psychology in Schools*, 2nd Edition. New York: Taylor & Francis; Marques, S. C., Lopez, S. J., and Pais-Ribeiro, J. L. (2009). 'Building hope for the future': A Program to foster strengths in middle school students. *Journal of Happiness Studies*. Retrieved from http://www.ofyp.umn.edu/ofypmedia/pdfs/highered/fye/bhf.pdf

flexibility to adjust in response to setbacks. C. R. Snyder, author of *The Psychology of Hope: You Can Get There from Here*, and Shane Lopez concur in identifying four steps in effective hopeful thinking: trusting that the future will be better than the present, believing one has the power to make it so, comprehending that there are multiple paths to each goal, and realizing that achieving them will not be free of obstacles.[11] Hence, to build hopeful students, have them write down their goals; this means identifying desires or aims—for instance, what they are hoping for or want to accomplish through academic learning.

Having students identify pathways is another part of the hope building process. Pathways reflect perceived ability to strategize to attain goals. A common method to assist students with developing pathways is to help them separate a larger goal, such as a career path into smaller subgoals, facilitating the identification of steps to be undertaken in a logical progression.[12] Hopeful students also may identify several routes or strategies to accomplish a desired goal and then choose the best one. Having alternative pathways available helps students to persevere in goal pursuit even when they encounter obstacles, as not all stumbling blocks can be surmounted.

Finally, hopeful students initiate agency; they identify the actions needed to act upon pathways toward attaining goals. The process enables students to view themselves as agents with the capacity to initiate—they have an "I can do this" attitude. Such agency is, furthermore, critical to adjusting or switching pathways when a strategy seems not to work.[13] However, pathways and agency—distinct components of hope—must work in tandem. Without pathways, the goal-pursuit process would become stagnant; without sufficiently motivating agency, no quantity of possible pathways will lead to goal attainment.[14] Therefore, out of hope flows cognitive processes entailing agency and pathways thinking, producing behaviors over time that tend to result in goal attainment.

Cultivating Hope

Hopeful students are more likely to be committed and determined to set and achieve academic goals; furthermore, guided experiences with goal setting (we discussed goal setting in Chapter 2) have been found to motivate adolescents to engage more hopefully in learning.[15] How can we preserve and cultivate students' perceptions and faith that they can shape their own goals and take responsibility for reaching them? We need to identify and bolster the assets and resources that help adolescents solve the problems that hinder their efforts. That is, we must help youth understand which of the components of hope—goals, pathways, or agency—they lack most and actively help them work diligently to realize their dreams.

A potent way for teachers to cultivate hope in young people is to integrate it directly into academic instruction. Researchers Susana Marques and Shane Lopez provide several research-based suggestions for infusing hope into lesson plans. For instance, in studying history students encounter an abundance of high-hope individuals; the hopefulness "process" can be illuminated by exploring their motivating goals, as well as the initiative and perseverance they used to overcome challenges and accomplish them. In language arts, personal narratives and short stories can illustrate and prompt discussion of the diverse roads driven by being hopeful. Physical education regularly should provide opportunities for students to understand their personal goals and tangibly measure movement toward them. And math is a key context in which the steps to foster hope can produce benefits in learning and reduce math anxiety.[16]

Ultimately, young adults build or reclaim hope through self-perceptions regarding competence to achieve goals by coping with obstacles that arise. Teachers wield great influence here: their communications, both verbal and subliminal, regarding students' academic potential, opportunities, and progress can reflect great expectations and confidence, fueling students' hopefulness. They must guide all their students to view both successes and failures as sources of encouragement to continue forward.

PROMOTING A SENSE OF PURPOSE

We promote a sense of purpose to help students build resilience to setbacks, boosting the motivation to learn despite obstacles. Generally, we help students understand how education is relevant to later educational, vocational, and life outcomes. Many students already believe that learning is important in an abstract sense; but to be motivated fully to engage, they also need to perceive that their learning can and will serve a purpose. We can help students understand that learning serves a purpose beyond economic self-interest—that learning also provides a compass in their search for significance as young adults, a guide toward the higher purpose of making a difference to society.

Purpose is intent or motivation to accomplish goals; personal meaning is the sense that one's life is significant and has direction. Together, a "sense of purpose" may be defined as the motivation that stimulates effort to progress toward personal goals.[17] Sense of purpose, therefore, helps students relate their schoolwork to paths in becoming their future selves, as well as to broader impacts that they may not fully envision yet.[18] The expectation of contributing to the community or serving as a positive example to others can sustain motivation at moments when foundational schoolwork may seem frustrating, or even boring. The sense of purpose is thus the attitude that counters the question "Why should I learn?" with the answer "Because all learning can lead to accomplishing meaningful ends, beyond the self." Thus, having a sense of purpose drives how much time, energy, and intensity students devote toward their education.[19]

Goal Setting

As does building hope in the classroom, promoting a sense of purpose depends upon guiding youth to set goals. Goal setting is a pursuit that enables students to think realistically about their future fulfillment of dreams and personal potential; at its most useful, it produces specific, even measurable, objectives for learning and life. We can teach students to view learning as a means to the end of achieving personally meaningful and socially purposeful objectives. Far from a trivial practical exercise, goal setting is a powerful component of ongoing motivation and leads ultimately to young people's longer-term commitment to and engagement in their own unfolding. Goal setting builds identity through non-passive participation in intentions about present and future, fulfilling the human need for autonomy. A sense of purpose, in turn, further motivates students to develop realistic plans for pursuing their goals, whether short- or long-term. Hence, self-articulated goals both reflect intrinsic motivations and further shape one's purpose in engaging in educational mandates and options.

As the section on building hope in the classroom explored, goal setting is linked to pathways and agency and thus work in tandem with promoting a sense of purpose. Furthermore, chosen goals lead to decisions about strategies and tools for organizing time and effort; therefore, clear and well-defined goals tend to increase students' persistence and self-efficacy and decrease their susceptibility to anxiety, disappointment, and frustration.[20] Students are more successful at relating goal setting, pursuit, and attainment to their enlarging sense of purpose if they have support from teachers. Teachers can help students acquire processes and strategies for goal progression. Goal articulation, prioritizing, self-monitoring, and delaying gratification—all these skills help young adults compete for global employment and obtain personally rewarding jobs. Open and honest discussions regarding alternative pathways and agency— whether and how to persevere, or whether to change tactics— help students stay on track to attaining their goals.

Service-Learning

We can better engage students' inherent desires to participate in meaningful roles and activities to develop their "future selves" by helping them find personal relevance in schooling. We provide opportunities for them to engage actively in service-learning activities; clearly, these lead toward consequential roles and responsibilities that improve society, especially their own communities.[21] This component, essential to pursuing educational equity, can be especially powerful for students whose families have been excluded from participating fully in American social, economic, and political life.[22]

Service-learning, an essential partnership method to promote a sense of purpose in the context of working toward personal goals, enables students to apply academic knowledge and skills to address real-world problems or needs in their own communities. Linking academic study to service-learning, its practical activities ideally remain tightly connected to learning objectives by contextualizing them. Service-learning produces powerful real-life experience; participating intelligently in giving back to the community enhances students' belief that they can contribute in meaningful ways to society. Connecting students to their own schools and to the real world, service-learning elevates their personal and social development toward a prosocial stance and enables them to collaborate with positive adult role models. In the process, youth acquire vocational skills and adult responsibility, build self-efficacy and self-esteem, and develop capacities for teamwork.[23]

Examples of service-learning include engaging in setting up a recycling program (linked to environmental science learning objectives), contributing to a charitable organization's fundraising efforts (economics), and testing water samples to document contamination (physical science). Participants in such opportunities readily develop critical thinking skills in real-world applications, plus leadership, communication, and collaboration skills.[24] All these dimensions of value added to school-based academics enhance students' growing senses of future-oriented and beyond-the-self purpose.

TEACHING STUDENTS SELF-CONTROL

Teaching students self-control (a.k.a. "self-regulation") is an important skill for all youth to possess, especially for those suffering stressors (e.g., trauma, struggles with anxiety, depression, suicidal ideation, and other psychological issues) to their social-emotional well-being. Students experiencing these stressors are subject to impairments or periodic struggles with executive functioning; executive functions (discussed in Chapter 2) are vital for academic learning and socioemotional development—as a matter of fact, we use these brain functions all the time.[25] Struggles with executive functioning ultimately impact the ability to exercise self-control; consequently, it becomes difficult for students to complete required classroom tasks or assignments and to make wise decisions.

Self-control is the capacity to override impulses or resist short-term desires in order to meet long-term goals. It is an important predictor or factor in the cultivation and enhancement of resilience and the reduction of psychological distress.[26] Central to the concept of self-control is the ability to override or change one's inner responses, as well as to interrupt undesired behavioral tendencies and refrain from acting on them. From this perspective, self-control contributes to producing a broad range of positive outcomes in life. In fact self-control is a good predictor of resilience; a resilient person has good control over impulses, the ability to delay gratification in regard to the potential consequences of her actions, and a belief in her abilities to manage life's challenges and situations effectively.[27] Essentially, individuals high in self-control may be more resilient to adversity because they are good at using cognitive reappraisal strategies aimed at changing the emotional meaning or relevance of an adverse situation, without changing it objectively, to make it less threatening.[28]

Research has shown that self-control predicts academic achievement and improvement more strongly than does measured intelligence.[29] Students' success, then, depends on how hard they work, how much they persist in the face of failure or obstacles, and how well they control their impulses. When students regulate themselves, they are able to manage their thoughts, actions, and emotions so they can realize goal attainment. In the long run, students with high self-control achieve better grades than impulsive students because they are better at getting tasks done on time, preventing leisure activities from interfering with getting their school work done, using study time effectively, and keeping emotional distractions from impairing their academic performance.[30] These outcomes are possible because self-controlled individuals are adept at regulating their behavioral, emotional, and attentional impulses to achieve long-term goals.[31] This is especially noteworthy, since findings show that self-control predicts income, savings, behavior, financial security, physical and mental health, and lack of criminal convictions in adulthood.[32] Similarly, these conclusions suggest that the individuals' ability to self-regulate enabled them to make decisions that led to positive life outcomes.

Young people can fall short of their academic potential if they do not learn to exercise self-control. But we can explicitly teach self-regulation, helping them to persist even amidst adversity or in the face of challenges so that they realize positive academic outcomes. Here are some helpful strategies to support young people's self-regulation abilities:

- Provide study skills instruction to help students access academic content; instruction will help students self-regulate and become more independent learners. These include skills that help students organize their materials, manage their time, stay on task, as well as read with comprehension, and retain and practice what is learned for use on later graded assignments.[33]

- Scaffold instruction by breaking learning into chunks and then providing a strategy or structure to make it easier for students to be able to accomplish each chunk of learning; this involves limiting the number of items to be learned at one time so that it is easier for students to process information. To scaffold instruction effectively, it is important to know what a student is capable of doing on his own—his zone of proximal development (ZPD), or the difference between what a learner can do independently and what he is able to do when provided with educational support. In short, determine what the learner understands and then modify the assignment within his ZPD.

- Help learners develop individualized SMART goals on areas that are important for and to them. Similar to the goal setting process in building hope and promoting sense of purpose, the SMART concept also provides students with a road map to tackle goals set for academic learning and beyond. Goals should be specific, measurable, attainable, results-focused, and achieved in a set time frame.[34] The process involves breaking goals down into smaller achievable steps, identifying how to measure progress, as well as naming and devising specific strategies and resources to use in overcoming obstacles. Realizing there is a time-frame to achieving goals, students monitor their progress to stay on track (with help from teachers).

- Give instruction on prioritizing tasks to support self-regulation. Prioritizing and tackling tasks builds students' ability to organize and manage their time. Prioritizing work not only makes it more manageable, but it also helps students to use their time more efficiently.[35] Instruction includes assisting students with detecting the difference between important, goal-oriented tasks (e.g., outlining information for a research paper that is due next week), and demanding, urgent tasks (e.g., writing an essay a student is behind on), as well as providing explanations about the different kinds of tasks, in terms of when, where, and how the work can be completed.[36]

- Model self-regulation to teach students how to manage their emotions so that their emotions do not hinder academic learning and performance. For example, a teacher can model by naming her emotions and attaching an emotional vocabulary word to illustrate how she is feeling (e.g., feeling frustrated about students talking when she is talking). Additionally, the teacher articulates how she processes her emotions so that students are able to learn the same skillset—the ability to handle emotions in safe, kind, and productive ways. Teaching students how to manage their emotions is a vital pathway to intellectual learning, as self-regulating feelings enables the brain to be able to receive learning and information.[37]

STRATEGIES TO FOSTER RESILIENT LEARNERS - A FRAMEWORK FOR SUPPORTING ACADEMIC SUCCESS: KEY POINTS

More and more students are coming to school with the stress of overwhelming adversity, trauma, and psychological issues that threaten to thwart their academic and life success. Therefore, we foster resilient learners who bounce back and maintain their motivation to learn even when facing challenges or encountering setbacks. In this chapter, we focused on these strategies:

- Build hope in the classroom by teaching students the three action-oriented components of hope: goal setting, pathways, and agency—all of which are necessary for goal attainment. Teachers integrate directly into their lesson plans methods that include exploring hopeful people, their goals, goal motivation, overcoming challenges to achieve goals, and measuring movement toward goal attainment.

- Promote youth's sense of purpose by guiding them to set goals and providing service-learning opportunities. Goal setting allows students to think realistically about their future fulfillment of dreams, and service-learning enables students to link and apply academic knowledge and skills to real-world problems and needs.

- Explicitly teach students self-control/self-regulation; strategies include providing study skills, scaffolding, SMART goal setting, prioritizing, and modeling to improve students' self-regulation skills. These strategies will help students make wise decisions that enable academic success and goal attainment.

> TEACHERS' COLLECTIVE ACTION IN SOLIDARITY WILL CONTRIBUTE TO BETTER STUDENT PERFORMANCE AND IMPROVED STUDENT OUTCOMES...

CHAPTER 5

Collaborate with a Community of Teacher Learners: Making a Strengths-Based Teaching Paradigm Happen

TEACHERS AND STUDENTS HAVE SIMILAR NEEDS: Just as students require caring relationships with their teachers, teachers need supportive relationships with their colleagues, in which they share ideas and solve problems together. This is especially vital for making a strengths-based paradigm happen, as teacher collaboration is part of the process. Collaboration occurs when a community of teacher learners work together to increase student learning and achievement. When educators come together and leverage their individual strengths toward becoming more impactful as a group, they can improve strengths-based teaching practices and focus on instructional issues that lead to improved student learning and achievement. Teachers' collective action in solidarity will contribute to better student performance and improved student outcomes, while simultaneously improving teacher job satisfaction and decreasing teacher turnover.[1] Thus, teachers develop authentic collaborative communities; they work together to accomplish and use communal resources to advance their skills, knowledge, and dispositions related to student learning without forfeiting accountability.[2]

Teachers collaborate within and across communities of teacher learners, emphasizing the importance of team effort or teamwork in helping young people achieve their learning potential (see Figure 5-1 for a collaboration inventory to assist with identifying the strengths and gaps in the collaborative environment at your school). The collaborative process provides opportunities to build relationships that provide mutual recognition and trust, thereby making it possible for teachers to work well together. The relationships are particularly vital for strengthening educators capacity to deliver holistic strengths-based instruction in collaboration with their colleagues.

PROFESSIONAL LEARNING COMMUNITIES FOR STRENGTHS-BASED TEACHING-LEARNING

Professional learning communities are a common and proven practice to promote teacher collaboration to enhance or expand teaching practices and effectiveness, ultimately to benefit the learning of each student. A professional learning community (PLC), a group of educators who take collective responsibility for student learning, share expertise and practice in an ongoing process of reflection, collaboration, inclusion, and in learning- and growth-oriented ways.[3] This team engages in a cycle of individual or collaborative learning, involving action research, data analysis, goal setting, and the implementation and modifications of teaching practices to meet the needs of all learners.[4] Ideally, all teachers will commit to incorporate the strengths-based philosophy: combining academic instruction with supporting students' social-emotional needs. They strive to develop skills in engaging students through their strengths and using dialogue about students from a strengths, not deficit perspective.

Specifically, the PLC can create opportunities for training to help teacher peers embrace and offer strengths-based teaching and learning to mitigate learning loss or instructional gaps, stimulate student's abilities, or address students' specific academic and social-emotional learning

FIGURE 5-1

Collaboration Inventory

| 0 Never | 1 Rarely | 2 Every now and then | 3 Often | 4 Very frequently or all the time |

☐ 1. Teachers at my school collaborate on how to best support students' academic and socioemotional needs to create and implement instructional plans linked to needs.

☐ 2. School leaders where I work invest time in establishing and maintaining a collaborative school environment, as well as set goals and expectations for meaningful collaboration.

☐ 3. My school creates the structures necessary for productive collaboration and addresses barriers that obstruct collaboration.

☐ 4. Teachers at my school regularly engage in routines where they communicate about classroom experiences to strengthen pedagogical practices in order to integrate social and emotional learning.

☐ 5. Teachers at my school engage with colleagues in a discussion focused on instructional issues and hold each other accountable for achieving goals or producing work products.

☐ 6. Teachers at my school engage in online reflective conversations between colleagues within and across schools, including debriefing classroom challenges (academic and socioemotional), receiving feedback on practices and identifying new pedagogical techniques to try.

☐ 7. Collaboration at my school is based on trust, commitment, open communication, and an appreciation for diverse ideas.

☐ 8. Administrators and teachers at my school work closely together to develop and select instructional materials, assessments, learning strategies, and plan for professional development.

☐ 9. During various collaboration meetings or opportunities at my school, my suggestions or points of view are considered by other teachers and the school administration.

☐ 10. Teachers at my school communicate and work with educational professionals in other roles, disciplines, and areas to facilitate mutual understanding and collective contributions to improve academic, social, and emotional outcomes for students.

Source: Adapted from Poulos, J., Culbertson, N., Piazza, P., & d'Entremont, C. (2014). Making Space: The Value of teacher collaboration. Rennie Center: Education Research and Policy.

needs. As a result, school professionals will enable students to build in self-understanding and insight and grow in self-confidence and in their true capacities to make informed decisions about their own learning.

Teacher communities collaborate in their efforts to make a strengths-based paradigm shift that would basically require them to overhaul their approach to teaching, transforming not only how they view and interact with their students, but also how they develop programs for and provide services to them as diverse individuals. The shift involves educators' understanding that young people's learning is dynamic and holistic, and that students learn and demonstrate their knowledge in different ways.[5] This may entail demonstrations of how to provide and mobilize supports and resources in ways that complement students' existing capacities, meanwhile enabling teachers to increase student performance and close gaps in achievement.

Teachers can accomplish a strengths-based teaching-learning culture through collaborative teaming or a PLC that consists of one or more teaming structures. These are just a few. Within a school or district, a PLC can be comprised of educators from various school districts in the same geographic region working together. Another PLC may include faculty members with similar responsibilities, for example, teachers from the same grade level or from the same subject area or comprised of faculty from different academic content areas. We will discuss further grade-level, subject-area, and peer-to-peer teams; besides ensuring continuity, these teaming structures make it easier to use the resources and expertise available in your own school, while cultivating teaching and learning practices that are strengths-based.

Grade-level teams can engage in collegial interactions that contribute to opportunities to improve student learning; educators can do so by using data to increase the school's academic rigor (e.g., interdisciplinary initiatives to foster critical thinking skills across all subject areas) and their ability to support student learning needs more effectively.[6] Subject-area and peer-to-peer teaming allow teachers to engage in meaningful collaborations to continuously improve their practices. In subject-area teams, teachers can address content area concerns; they get to use each other as resources on strengths-based pedagogical challenges. Educators rely on the expertise of their peers to develop a holistic understanding of student learning (e.g., garnering insights about gaps in student mastery of a particular skill or concept).[7] In peer-to-peer interactions (also called teacher-to-teacher mentoring), dialogue is more specific to a teacher's concern about classroom practice—for example, these involve teaching observations, providing or getting feedback, or adjusting pedagogy to meet student needs. Peer-to-peer teaming works for all teachers, as it is carried out for the sake of continuous improvement.

Establishing and maintaining a PLC is doable but not easily realized—generally because of time constraints. Even if teacher teams share the same planning period, there is not much free time to meet at school. I noticed this challenge in the high schools where I taught. Specifically, in one of the schools, school administrators fostered and supported a collaborative workplace for teachers. One PLC formation or collaborative team consisted of teachers of the same grade level and subject area. Administrators ensured we teachers shared the same planning period so that we had structured time to work together in planning instruction, and we were generally given a block of time on teacher planning days. Even with the opportunities provided, we concluded that collaboration did not come without cost—without sacrificing some of the time each of us needed to complete our own individual responsibilities. Therefore, our team—facilitated by a trained teacher leader—decided that we would have a longer meeting time on a scheduled day of the week combined with our reaching out to one another electronically. This option provided us with more chances for collaborative inquiry—to share ideas and expertise, discuss specific lesson plans, the curriculum, student achievement data, and behavior, as well as dialogue about innovative ways to ensure student success and learn from one another. Beyond these opportunities, we also observed one another's classrooms and shared feedback contributing to an increased understanding of the content that we taught and the role we played in helping all students achieve. As noted by research, in our collegial relationship we felt less isolated when we leveraged our individual strengths to create coherence across our classrooms and share responsibility for student learning.[8] In essence, my professional capacity to provide quality instruction grew in a community of teacher learners.

BUILDING COLLABORATION IN TEACHER COMMUNITIES

Having a teaming structure in place does not guarantee that any collaborative activities will take place or even that effective collaboration occurs in teacher communities. Effective teacher collaboration is defined as engaging in regular routines where teachers communicate about classroom experiences in an effort to strengthen pedagogical expertise.[9] To engage in purposeful collaboration, teachers must build relationships with one another to create a platform that enables them to advance their learning, foster collegiality, decrease teacher isolation, and lead them to greater insights about teaching and learning, ultimately contributing to improved student learning.[10] And if done correctly, collaborations among fellow educators can save time, reduce stress, and inspire innovative lessons.

Teacher teams must intentionally work to achieve effective collaboration; it can be realized if they employ these strategies:[11]

- Create a shared vision of caring for students and their learning (i.e.; a vision involving the perspective that youth are competent and capable learners with unique qualities and abilities); set goals related to the vision to establish a sense of ownership.

- Develop a sense of community by taking the time to get to know colleagues, understand their interests, learning styles, and needs to connect with them on a personal level.

- Identify and establish norms for the team; these include defining roles and responsibilities, using protocols for interpersonal communication, and outlining parameters for time management.
- Use discussion for the purpose of stating opinions, building consensus or making decisions; use dialogue to cultivate deep professional learning by inviting multiple perspectives, exploring biases and assumptions, questioning the status quo, and entertaining new ways of knowing and being.

Additional criteria for facilitating effective collaboration have been proposed by Vangrieken and colleagues:[12]

- Actively keep track of innovations or developments in the education world.
- Be flexible with pedagogical approaches.
- Put forth an adequate amount of effort toward collaboration.
- Possess adequate competencies: knowledge, skills, and strategies to engage in collaborative work; use all team members' expertise.

By doing so, collaboration effectiveness is more likely to lead to the attainment of team-set goals, the increase of knowledge and its application to improve team members' practice, and the translation of knowledge into actual change to classroom practices.

IMPORTANCE OF RELATIONAL INTELLIGENCE IN IMPROVING COLLABORATION

Collaborating with and learning from peers to make a holistic strengths-based ideology happen does not come without challenges; consequently, it is necessary that teachers develop relational intelligence, so that they learn how to work together. This involves building relationships with other teachers to develop comfort in sharing ideas and concerns, asking questions or asking for advice, and offering solutions. Relational intelligence is the ability to perceive and mentally process information, assess risk, and perceive cause and effect in ways that enable one to learn, gain insight, and capitalize on the dynamics of individual and group relationships.[13] The skill involves cultivating relational self-awareness: having a sense of how one behaves, how one is perceived, and how one perceives his relationships are with others.[14] Relational awareness also includes an understanding of what one's role is on a collaborative team as well as the recognition of the fundamental importance of complementarity in the communal relationship. In schools complementarity is the understanding that a teacher can be what she is and do what she can do because somebody else is fulfilling a role or part that she is not; in the relationship, the qualities of one team member supplement or enhance the different qualities of others on the team.[15]

Relational intelligence consists of learned or acquired skills that endow educators with the ability to sustain relationships through collaboration—these interactions with coworkers are to increase student learning. In short, relational skills will empower teachers with a competitive advantage, as they will be enabled to develop helpful and supportive relationships with teacher peers from various cultural backgrounds, interests, and values; they will be allowed to connect and act interpersonally and be ethically competent.[16] In this way, relational intelligence acts as a catalyst for community-building and relationship cultivation among teacher colleagues, which, in turn, also helps with teacher engagement, retention, performance, and well-being.[17]

Relational intelligence is an evolution of emotional intelligence, mainly in the areas of empathy and social skills—both of which are complimentary to interpersonal intelligence. Empathy is the ability to recognize emotions in others, and social skills consist of the ability to manage relationships. Essentially, to possess relational intelligence, one must first have emotional intelligence.[18] Emotional intelligence is our ability as humans to manage emotions, to carry out accurate reasoning about emotions, and to process emotional information to enhance our thoughts, guide our actions, and understand interpersonal dynamics.[19] In other words, the ability to understand and manage our emotions and those of others (emotional intelligence) expands and develops our ability to relate better to others and build trusting relationships (relational intelligence).

Educators can build relational intelligence to improve collaborative connections at an individual and group level; those who learn to genuinely connect and develop relational (interpersonal) intelligence contribute to a culture of engagement and enhanced team dynamics and collaboration. To illustrate, it is expected that team members will bring diverse expertise and their own views on how to approach or make a strengths-based approach to instruction a reality; however, members with interpersonal intelligence skills can help forge the connections that act as a bridge from one team member's approach to a problem to another's approach, providing the development of mutual trust to overcome the problem.[20] Relational or interpersonal intelligence will allow teachers to generate better and more innovative ideas as well as develop a stronger sense of shared meaning and purpose.[21]

Teachers need to be able to connect with each other, relate better to one another, and collaborate with sensitivity to coworkers of diverse backgrounds and personalities. As educators develop the skills to build collaborative relationships with their peers, they will be better able to model and instruct students who also need to develop the skills to collaborate with other students and teachers of different backgrounds and perspectives. Hence, teachers need intelligence about relationships so that their interactions can contribute to productive collaboration. They need interpersonal skills that allow them to relate to one another properly; these include the ability to establish trust, communicate effectively, engage in active listening, manage and resolve conflict, and employ perspective taking and empathy.

Establish Trust

It is important for educators to develop relational intelligence to build the trust required for productive collaboration. In the context of teamwork and collaboration, trust is confidence among colleagues that their peers' intentions are good, and that there is no reason to be protective or careful around them.[22] That is, teachers need psychological safety to engage in teamwork and to build trusting relationships with their colleagues; they need to believe that their coworkers are trustworthy—that it is safe to come to them for support or guidance and the encouragement needed for them to succeed. As Stephen Covey asserts in his book *The Speed of Trust: The One Thing That Changes Everything*, nothing is more impactful on people, their work, and their performance than trust; it is the "one thing that has the potential to create unparalleled success and prosperity in every dimension of life."[23] Hence, building sustainable and trustful connections is requisite for developing collaborative working relationships with teacher peers.

It takes courage and humility to trust colleagues, as teachers must get comfortable being vulnerable with one another and be confident that their respective vulnerabilities (e.g., skill deficiencies, interpersonal shortcomings, requests for help) will not be used against them.[24] However, when colleagues trust each other, they plan more effectively, work more efficiently, and become a stronger community of teacher learners. Teachers can engage in the following strategies to establish trust in their collaborative teams:[25]

- Encourage honesty and open communication or dialogue. Team members share honest opinions and feedback, opening up the way for better ideas and stronger outputs.
- Establish opportunities for creative collaboration to occur. To grow trust, teacher peers have to learn to solve problems together (teams get creative and resourceful) and rely on each other to improve an issue such as low student performance.

- Work together as a self-organized team. A team such as this creates a structure in which it is more self-directed; team members learn to trust each other more and to make decisions together.
- Keep roles and responsibilities clear. This is one of the best ways to get people to trust each other. Each member understands his role and responsibilities as well as those of his colleagues.
- Make feedback a regular part of team culture. Feedback from peers should help each teacher grow individually and teacher teams grow as a whole; seeing the growth boosts overall team trust.

The intent is to have a community of teachers who align to celebrate individual and collective strengths, focus on improvement and goal setting, and share accountability for student learning.[26] It is in this climate of trust that educators build a cohesive community and create the safe environment that is necessary for effective communication.

Communicate Effectively

Communication, ways of sending and receiving messages, is a valuable way to build trust among teacher colleagues; the messages may be exchanged in words, gestures, facial expressions, and behaviors.[27] Communication is both verbal and non-verbal and is influenced by factors such as age, gender, race, and ethnicity. With this information in mind, teacher colleagues can operate from the understanding that their coworkers have various experiences that inform their world view, impacting the different ways they communicate. However, the goal of effective communication is to be understood, to be able to listen to others, and be able to convey thoughts and feelings.[28] It involves the sharing or exchanging of information (e.g., about student learning and teacher practices), while also enabling relationships to function successfully; effective functioning of relationships can boost teamwork and lead to better collaboration and productivity.[29] Simply put, collaborative relationships will not take place without effective communication. Thus, the more successful communication is, the better the connection will be between collegial teams, because they will be able to exchange knowledge and ideas to pursue the goal of implementing teaching-learning that is strengths-based. Other byproducts of efficacious communication include increased productivity, improved stakeholder alignment, higher employee engagement, and reduced turnover.[30]

Communication channels are a critical part of supporting effective team collaboration; the channels (verbal, emails, video conferencing, etc.) provide the means for fruitful interactions to occur. Using the correct channels when communicating will help team members feel more connected and contribute to the likelihood that they work productively on tasks to improve teaching practices to benefit student learning.[31] When communicating verbally, a school professional should steer the conversation with clarity, using words that connect with others. In addition, his communication tone should encourage an exchange of ideas—a tone that speaks with passion. In this way, effective communication can minimize errors, as well as ensure team members understand their tasks and that they are up to date on improvement strategies.[32] Consequently, collaborative teams should also instill norms for communication that value constructive criticism as a vehicle for improvement and learning from colleagues; the idea is for teachers to be able to accept constructive feedback so that they can act on input from their peers to complete tasks or achieve outcomes.[33]

Engage in Active Listening

Understanding how to collaborate and communicate involves active listening. Active listening refers to a set of listening skills that encompasses listening, paying attention to body language or nonverbal cues, summarizing and paraphrasing, and asking follow-up, clarifying, and probing questions.[34] Sometimes called empathic or reflective listening, active listening allows individuals to build and strengthen relationships, as listening to others shows care and concern about what they have to say and how they feel. Good listeners develop a greater understanding of what is being communicated emotionally and intellectually; this helps to reduce tension and create a safe environment conducive to collaborative problem solving. Thus, when team members truly listen to each other, they express their ongoing regard for one another, building the trust and understanding that allows them to collaborate effectively.[35]

Active listening can occur when the listener resists the urge to think about his reply while the other person is speaking, or even responding before fully understanding the other person's thoughts; instead, the listener waits and then asks questions to draw out more details without giving the impression of "grilling" the speaker.[36] This can be accomplished when the speaker avoids making assumptions and refrains from giving advice. As a result, the listener is enabled to receive and accurately interpret the speaker's message in order to provide an appropriate response; this is critical to the success of effective collaboration, communication, and conflict management and resolution.[37]

Manage and Resolve Conflict

Relationship building does not discourage conflict itself but rather encourages the safety to challenge ideas and work through conflict.[38] Conflict, an inevitable part of life, refers to any situation in which people have incompatible interests, goals, principles, or feelings. It is ultimately based on perceptions and exists whenever one individual believes that his interests or goals are being opposed or negatively affected by another. It is not unusual for relational conflicts to arise among teacher colleagues, as collaborative teams are comprised of multiple personalities and individuals with unique views, values, and belief systems. Relationship conflicts may also arise from poor communication, underdeveloped skills in interacting with others, stereotyping, misconceptions, and time constraints. Other factors include misunderstandings of group norms, confusion over language and communication styles, or underlying trust is missing, ultimately resulting in poor teacher collaboration.[39] Conflict can generate negative feelings that disrupt collaboration; it can discourage coworkers engaged in a dispute from sharing resources and collaborating with each other.[40] Therefore, it must be managed or resolved so that it does not destroy trust among colleagues but lead to learning and growth, while maintaining supportive working relationships.[41]

Managing conflict implies that the conflict exists, but it is controlled in such a way that the conflict is not a major problem to collegial collaboration. Case in point, dialogue allows teacher coworkers to collaborate successfully, enabling them to share and broaden knowledge. However, dialogue may also lead to conflict that needs to be managed. It can be helpful for teacher teams to develop a conflict management plan and to monitor conflict as it arises. Teams can help manage conflict by providing time, space, grace, and support for their peers as they work through their emotions. Individuals also should monitor their own emotions and practice self-care. Using professional judgment, collaborative teams can determine when to explore the roots of conflict and when to provide space for reflection and cooling down, especially since conflict may come even in the face of constructive feedback. And while sometimes uncomfortable, conflict often provides opportunities for growth and can lead to creative solutions to problems.[42]

Some incompatible colleague interactions can be resolved instead of managed. Resolving conflict means that some end or solution to the problem has been determined. In this case, teams work together to arrive at constructive solutions while maintaining positive working relationships; they explore common and opposing options to reach mutually acceptable positive solutions. In any workplace, ideas will collide at some point or another. When there is a problem, teachers can assertively seek facilitation, mediation, or creative solutions to resolve conflicts. This involves the ability to clarify a particular dispute, listen in a nonjudgmental way to multiple perspectives, evaluate why the conflict has arisen, and offer suggestions for reaching an equitable compromise.[43] Using a collaborative approach such as this is more likely to protect productive relationships. This can occur when team members' acknowledge that not everyone will be satisfied by the solution or outcome; therefore, members reach the conclusion to "let go" and move on to more collaborative issues.[44] Hence, the expectation is that teachers will not agree about everything because they have diverse personalities, opinions, and are all uniquely different. However, to resolve or manage many relationship conflicts, teams can learn to employ empathy and perspective-taking skills to relate better when interacting collaboratively.

Employ Perspective Taking and Empathy

Perspective taking and empathy are critical for developing the relational intelligence skills for successful collaborative relationships. Perspective taking is the ability to take someone else's viewpoint into account when thinking; perceiving a situation or understanding a concept from another's point of view mitigates conflicts for more successful relationship building, meanwhile keeping tension low for a more pleasant atmosphere.[45] When teacher colleagues try to understand the perspectives of their team members and share their feelings, they may be better able to accept opinions different than their own to achieve mutually beneficial outcomes. Additionally, perspective taking enables teachers to respect not only the abilities each colleague brings to the team, but also allows them to accept discussion or multiple viewpoints and disagreement; taking the perspective of others is a key ingredient in the reduction of interpersonal conflict and in the formation, maintenance, and preservation of interpersonal relationships.[46]

Perspective taking generally triggers empathy; empathy is the ability to understand and comprehend the emotions and behavior of another person beyond background or differences in belief. It involves connecting with others, building relationships, listening to, and caring for others. This skill allows us to step imaginatively into another person's place, understanding his feelings, thoughts, and perspectives, and then using that understanding as a compass to navigate interpersonal relationships.[47] Understanding does not mean agreement with the person's feelings or point of view but instead means acceptance that the perspective is different than one's own. In this way, teachers employ empathy, allowing them to become culturally sensitive and enabling them to develop skills in maintaining positive collaborative relationships with their diverse peers.[48] Empathy builds the openness necessary for effective collaboration with others from different backgrounds and experiences; in other words, to collaborate effectively teacher peers would need to listen and respond to dissimilar perspectives with generosity, patience, and understanding, as well as establish a welcoming space for colleagues to share their ideas without fear of judgment.[49] Thus, successful collaboration is fueled by empathy; though empathic collaboration often involves voicing opposing opinions and creating moments of tension for team members, these moments frequently provide team members with impactful ideas that lead to creative problem solving.[50]

STRATEGIES TO COLLABORATE WITH A COMMUNITY OF TEACHER LEARNERS – MAKING A STRENGTHS-BASED TEACHING PARADIGM HAPPEN: KEY POINTS

A community of teacher learners can work together to make strengths-based teaching-learning a reality in the classroom and improve their professional capacity to increase student learning and achievement. In collaborative communities, teachers are provided with the opportunity for equitable dialogue and decision making. In this chapter, we explored these strategies:

- Committing to continuous improvement, educators connect in professional learning communities of different types, including grade-level, subject-area, and peer-to-peer teams. Teachers share resources, information, and expertise by tapping into the perspectives of diverse colleagues.

- To build productive collaboration, a community of teachers create a shared vision and set goals connected to it, establish norms, use discussion and dialogue for consensus building and decision making, adapt approaches and make suitable changes, put forth effort in collaborative work, and use the expertise of all team members.

- Educators improve collaboration through relational intelligence; these restorative skills—establishing trusting relationships, ensuring effective communication by listening carefully, managing and resolving conflicts quickly, and engaging in perspective taking and empathy—help teacher colleagues connect with and relate to each other better.

> REFLECTION WILL SUPPORT TEACHERS IN SHIFTING TO AND DEEPLY UNDERSTANDING STRENGTHS-BASED TEACHING-LEARNING STRATEGIES.

CHAPTER 6

Engage in Continuous Reflection: Bolstering Teachers' Strengths-Based Teaching-Learning Practices

To grow, individuals engage in reflection, or give serious thought and consideration to develop a deeper understanding of the decisions they need to make or actions they must undertake to be successful. Reflection is a vital part of teaching and learning and an essential part of professional development and improvement. Reflection allows teachers to develop continually the necessary skills, knowledge, and approaches to achieve the best outcomes for students; the teacher challenges assumptions of everyday practice and critically evaluate his own responses to teaching practices.[1] Thus, reflection encompasses the cognitive process of constantly thinking about, and monitoring one's practice in conjunction with consideration of existing knowledge about teaching so that practice can continually be improved.[2]

Reflection will support teachers in shifting to and deeply understanding strengths-based teaching-learning strategies (see Figure 6-1 for a self-reflection tool). The goal of the strategies—building teacher-student connections to improve learning, cultivating self-regulated learning to improve engagement and performance, tapping into youths' cognitive abilities using the multiple intelligences approach, and fostering resilient learners to support academic success—is to provide a restorative approach, enhancing students' acquisition of knowledge and skills and ultimately providing an equitable education. Through ongoing critical reflection, teachers shape their own development through self-observation and self-evaluation, contributing to both continual self-improvement and teacher quality.[3] Educators can utilize various strategies to practice reflection to bolster teaching methods, while enabling them to adjust and improve continuously.

STRATEGIES TO PRACTICE REFLECTION

As it is with understanding and executing any new teaching practices, reflection is crucial to implementation and mastery of strengths-based teaching methods. The first step in the process of reflection is gathering information about what happens in the classroom.[4] Here are some ways to capture the data needed to practice reflection:

- **Journaling** - Writing can be an excellent tool for teachers to develop and hone their reflective skills for "doing and analyzing what they do";[5] this process of reflection is purely personal. After each lesson teachers can write notes on what did or did not go well in the classroom. Through journaling, teachers can gain clarity on their thinking as well as enable ideas and insights to take hold. Notes may consist of existing instructional delivery or execution issues, proof of progress from students (evidence of learning), and materials or approaches needed to make a lesson better.[6] Hence, journaling provides the practitioner with a better understanding of where to focus efforts for improvements and helps build resilience, which is particularly important, given the current teaching landscape.[7]

- **Peer observation** – A teacher can invite a colleague to come into his class (observation may also be done virtually) to collect information about the lesson and student engagement. Peer observations work best with guiding questions to form the focus of the observation, particularly since the colleague will be giving feedback. The teacher identifies what she wants to reflect on; however, it is better to focus and collect data on one strategy or practice in one lesson or one class period. The colleague should give detailed and thought-provoking information or feedback, providing a rich data source to help inform the teacher's deep reflection.[8] Structured reflection of this type will allow the observing teacher to watch her peer implement instructional strategies such as strengths-based teaching. Together, the teachers reflect on what they see and identify the components of the lesson that contributed to its success.

- **Video-based reflection** – Studies show that using video to reflect upon teaching practice improves teacher quality and student achievement. Video-based reflection provides an unaltered and unbiased point of reference;[9] a teacher can observe and think about her own performance, identifying both strengths and weaknesses to get a clear understanding of what and where she needs to improve. In addition, video reflection is a resource for engaging in critical dialogue with other educators about instructional practices and the learning process.

- **Student feedback** – We can reflect by having students give us anonymous feedback. This involves asking them questions about a specific lesson (e.g., What can I do differently in this lesson to help you learn better?) or asking them to give us ideas about approaches that would aid in better developing their understanding and skills;[10] student feedback can also be gathered through simple questionnaires. In the process, we can bolster our strengths-based teaching practices, add different and valuable perspectives, and learn and grow as educators.

FIGURE 6-1
Strengths-Based Teaching-Learning Strategies - Self-Reflection Tool

Strategy 1: Employ strengths-based teaching-learning to build connections with students that improve learning		
<ul><li>I implement learning experiences to affirm students' strengths to help them achieve at their highest capacity.</li><li>I engage students as partners or active members in the learning process.</li><li>I make certain all students feel a sense of belonging in my classroom.</li><li>I build trust with students to improve my connections with them.</li><li>I incorporate culturally responsive teaching to build rapport with the diverse students in my classroom.</li><li>As a culturally responsive teacher, I display cultural competence, practice cultural humility, and engage in perspective taking to create bonds with my students.</li></ul>		
Strengths	Opportunities for Improvement	Next Steps
Strategy 2: Cultivate self-regulated learning to support academic engagement and performance		
<ul><li>I support my students' academic engagement and performance by teaching them how to learn.</li><li>I guide my students to self-regulated learning by integrating goal setting instruction, giving feedback, and providing opportunities for student self-reflection.</li><li>I use various strategies to strengthen students' executive functioning skills to support their academic engagement and performance.</li><li>I develop students' self-regulatory skills by teaching metacognitive strategies.</li></ul>		
Strengths	Opportunities for Improvement	Next Steps

Strategy 3: Tap into youths' cognitive abilities, using the multiple intelligences approach to accelerate learning

- I incorporate the multiple intelligences theory/approach to help students understand their cognitive and metacognitive abilities.
- I assess my students' existing multiple intelligences strengths to build from their existing cognitive skills and to help them come to a better understanding of how their minds learn.
- I include at least eight different pathways for students to learn or process information.
- I incorporate authentic assessments to evaluate student learning.

Strengths	Opportunities for Improvement	Next Steps

Strategy 4: Foster resilient learners to support academic success

- I encourage students to use their emotional and behavioral strengths to cope with academic and life challenges.
- I use a hope building process that includes having students write goals, identify strategies to achieve goals, and name the actions they would use to sustain application of those strategies.
- I cultivate hope in my students by integrating it directly into instruction.
- I promote students' sense of purpose by making learning relevant to real life, as well as to later educational, vocational, and life outcomes.
- I provide service-learning opportunities to help students work toward personal and academic goals, enabling them to apply academic knowledge and skills to address real-world problems.
- I explicitly teach self-regulation/self-control strategies to support students' academic success.

Strengths	Opportunities for Improvement	Next Steps

After capturing the data, teachers analyze and monitor their thinking and understanding to develop their capacity for practice. In this way, teachers move from experiencing teaching methods to understanding how they are beneficial for student learning and achievement.[11]

REFLECTIVE PRACTICE AND STRENGTHS-BASED TEACHING-LEARNING

On the road to learning recovery, teachers want to ensure students are provided with rigorous work. In light of the disruptions to schooling due to pandemic-related factors, teachers have noticed that students have lost their confidence in their ability to grapple with cognitively demanding assignments. Consequently, it is difficult to grow students' capacity for deeper learning; teachers would need to provide more scaffolding to develop students' capacity to turn learning into usable knowledge.[12] One way to do this is to teach metacognitive strategies (recall that we discussed metacognition in Chapter 2); we help students become aware of how they learn so they are able to regulate and monitor their own learning processes. By teaching at this level, we are giving students increased self-confidence and the gift of lifelong learning.[13]

Now let's assume that you want to accelerate learning for students so they are capable of handling rigorous work. You decide to teach them metacognitive strategies. Suppose your first lesson did not go well—perhaps many of the students did not understand your explanation about how to monitor their own learning, so you need to think about what you said and why your explanation may have been unclear. To improve your practice, you can turn this struggle into reflective questions like these:[14]

- How can I explicitly teach metacognitive strategies, model their use, and incorporate the strategies in my lessons?
- How may I encourage students to reflect on the strategies they use to complete assignments, and to identify which learning strategies are most effective for them?

- How can I assist my students with identifying their own learning goals, as well as planning, monitoring, and evaluating their own learning?
- How can my professional learning community support building my knowledge and skills in using metacognitive strategies?

In the reflective practice process, the educator is afforded the opportunity to gain new insights about himself, his underlying beliefs, and a strengths-based teaching method such as metacognitive strategies instruction—a self-regulated learning strategy to enhance student learning, engagement, and performance. In the process of teaching metacognitive strategies, the educator uses guided questions to self-assess the effect of his teaching on learning in order to consider new ways of providing instruction to improve student learning. Afterwards, he will try these ideas in practice. Of course, the process is cyclical; it will be repeated again because self-reflection never stops.[15] Thus, reflective practice facilitates teaching, learning, and understanding, thereby making it crucial to teachers' professional development.[16]

A reflective teacher also participates in critical dialogue or reflections with others. In a professional learning community and/or with leaders, teachers can discuss how best to incorporate strengths-based teaching methods in their practices. In this way, reflective practice creates an environment of collaboration as teachers question and adapt both their own practice and that of their colleagues. When teachers team up, draw on expertise, and offer each other support, this results in a more productive working environment.[17] Engaging in reflective practice with colleagues, though, is more effective when teachers are able to establish good working relationships (see Chapter 5 for a more in depth discussion of forming collaborative working relationships). It is in an atmosphere of supportive and constructive but honest feedback that educators build the capability to quickly identify areas for improvement and to develop collaboratively the best ways for moving forward.[18] Hence, teachers will engage in reflective practice to support their implementation of strengths-based teaching methods. Through sustained support and guidance from their colleagues, teachers not only build knowledge and skills, but they are also empowered to participate in professional development more fully through reflection, evaluation, and revision of their pedagogical approaches.

Reflection can also be used to set goals. To encourage effective reflective practice, each teacher can create an instructional development plan that involves a goal connected to how to improve student achievement. For instance, creating specific and measurable goals connected to the implementation of strengths-based teaching-learning practices will support teachers' implementation and understanding of the methods, likely increasing the probability of sustained changes to instructional practices. As with any goal, a plan for execution is necessary; it indicates exactly what you will do differently, how you will do it differently, what resources and support you need, who you will seek guidance from, and how you will monitor and reflect on the learning impact. A small, specific, and measurable goal—or no more than three goals—will allow for monitoring and reflecting on progress. Nonetheless, a written instructional development plan should be created for each goal; the plan includes an implementation approach, method for monitoring and reflecting, and expected educator learning outcomes.[19]

STRATEGIES TO ENGAGE IN CONTINUOUS REFLECTION - BOLSTERING TEACHERS' STRENGTHS-BASED TEACHING LEARNING PRACTICES: KEY POINTS

Continuous reflection will support teachers in shifting to strengths-based teaching-learning practices, as it is with understanding and executing any other new teaching practices. The emphasis in this chapter is on these tactics:

- To engage in continuous reflection, teachers first gather data about what happens in the classroom to support their knowledge of executing strengths teaching methods in the classroom. They employ various strategies that include journaling, peer observation, video-based reflection, and student feedback to enable continuous improvement. These contribute to a teacher's participation in reflective practice, a cyclical, systematic process of collecting, recording, and analyzing thoughts and observations about teaching and learning.

- Teachers participate in reflective practice to develop their capacity to deliver strengths-based teaching and learning strategies. They do so through both a personal process and one that involves critical dialogue or reflections with colleagues. Another way to encourage reflective practice is to have teachers construct an instructional development plan that involves creating specific, measurable goals.

> AT THE HEART OF THE STRATEGIES IS CAREFUL ATTENTION TO ESTABLISHING AUTHENTIC TEACHER-STUDENT AND TEACHER-TEACHER RELATIONSHIPS.

Conclusion:
Strengths-Based Teaching-Learning:
Paving an Equitable Way Forward

PRE-PANDEMIC RESEARCH INFORMS US THAT DISENGAGEMENT, socioemotional well-being issues, and loss of hope for the future comprise some of the biggest challenges impeding optimal student performance.[1] These same challenges, exposed and exacerbated by the pandemic, are also relevant to the current educational landscape. Thus, we haven an urgent need for a strengths-based approach to education. Research indicates that the method provides a solid foundation for building hope in students and fortifying their engagement in learning.[2] Furthermore, it takes into consideration student learning as well as the noneducational issues that critically interfere with optimal learning and life success, acknowledging the interconnectedness of academic success and social-emotional health.

A strengths lens to teaching and learning is a valuable addition to the variety of strategies available to educators desiring to embrace a restorative approach to nurture the whole child. The philosophy recognizes and addresses each student's unique strengths, needs, and interests, while also providing a practical method to address the distinct aspirations and cultural backgrounds of individual students. At the heart of the strategies is careful attention to establishing authentic teacher-student and teacher-teacher relationships. Hence, the perspective is most useful in attending to long-standing inequities, while supporting the academic, cognitive, and socioemotional growth of all students.

We intentionally develop youth's intellectual or cognitive strengths as well as their socioemotional capabilities to help them become more involved with and enthusiastic about school and the opportunities it presents for their personal growth. Students are enabled to 1) build in self-understanding and insight, as they grow in self-confidence and in their true capacities to make informed academic decisions, 2) develop the ability to self-regulate or direct their own learning, and 3) build resilience in the face of adversity, while also improving their socioemotional competence.

Our young people's strengths will support them in improving their performance and accelerating the learning process for them. Acceleration does not necessarily mean going faster, but it does mean that we provide the right supports to enable students to take on rigorous academic work. This universal intervention is designed to assist teachers in their efforts to move students forward. Educators will be able to support both struggling and on-track students—students with a wide range of learning needs.

To review, strengths-based teaching-learning outlines six essential strategies. The first four focus on instructional practices that benefit the whole student, and the last two outline practices that build teachers' professional capacity to support the philosophy. Together, these elevate the development of all students, ultimately providing restorative practices to advance educational equity:

1. to employ strengths-based teaching-learning practices to build connections with students that improve student learning, focusing on cultivating students' sense of belonging and building relational trust, while also incorporating culturally responsive pedagogy to improve rapport by building cultural competence, practicing cultural humility, and engaging in perspective taking;

2. to cultivate self-regulated learning to support academic engagement and performance through a focus on using goal setting, feedback, and self-reflection to teach students how to learn; with specific attention to executive functions and metacognition as valuable self-regulatory processes to scaffold student learning;

3. to tap into students' cognitive abilities by examining the multiple intelligences (MI) theory as a framework for understanding cognitive and metacognitive abilities, while also assessing students' existing MI, developing MI abilities in the classroom, and using authentic assessments to evaluate student learning;

4. to foster resilient learners by building hope in the classroom, promoting a sense of purpose, and teaching students self-control/self-regulation so that they realize academic success despite dealing with adversity or other challenging life situations;

5. to build educators' professional capacity to collaborate with a community of teacher learners who will make a strengths-based teaching paradigm happen, as they improve collaboration by developing relational intelligence skills: establishing trust, communicating effectively, engaging in active listening, managing and resolving conflict, and employing perspective taking and empathy; and

6. to build teachers' professional ability to engage in ongoing reflection to support their implementation of strengths-based teaching and learning practices by focusing on various strategies to participate in a personal reflection process or in reflections with colleagues and further encouraging reflective practice through the construction of instructional development plans.

Hopefully, this book empowers teachers to incorporate strengths-based teaching-learning strategies in ways that are beneficial to students' development, helping us to rebuild stronger our public education system. The strategies presented provide a game plan for educators wanting to fortify a curriculum already demanding academic rigor and also offer a plan for mitigating gaps in skills development as a result of pandemic-related disruptions or other hindrances to student learning. In this way, we recalibrate and grow from adversity, progressing toward educational equity in a manner that treats each student as an intact, whole individual.

Endnotes

Introduction

[1] Gewertz, C. (2022). Students train to spot peers with mental health struggles and guide them to help. Education Week. Retrieved from https://www.edweek.org/leadership/students-train-to-spot-peers-with-mental-health-struggles-and-guide-them-to-help/2022/03

Jones, T. M., Williford, A., Spencer, M. S., Riggs, N. R., Toll, R., George, M., Becker, K., & Bruick, S. (2021). School Mental Health Providers' Perspectives on the Impact of COVID-19 on Racial Inequities and School Disengagement. *Children & Schools*, cdab009. https://doi.org/10.1093/cs/cdab009

[2] Lopez, S. J. & Louis, M. C. (2009). The Principles of strengths-based education. *Journal of College and Character*, 10(4).

[3] Resiliency Initiatives (2011). *Embracing a Strengths-Based Perspective and Practice in Education*. Retrieved from http://www.mifras.org/know/wp-content/uploads/2017/01/Strengths-BasedSchoolCultureAndPractice.pdf

[4] Lopez, S. J. & Louis, M. C. (2009), *op. cit.*

[5] Lopez, S. J. (2013). *Making hope happen: Create the future you want for yourself and others*. New York: Simon & Schuster.

Snyder, C. R. (1994). *The Psychology of hope: You can get there from here*. New York: The Free Press.

[6] Lopez, S. J., Rose, S., Robinson, C., Marques, S. C., & Pais-Ribeiro, J. (2014). Measuring and promoting hope in schoolchildren. In M. J. Furlong, R. Gilman, and E. S. Huebner (Eds.), *Handbook of positive psychology in schools, 2nd edition*. New York: Taylor & Francis.

[7] The Vermont-NEA Racial Justice Task Force (2015). Restorative practices. Retrieved from http://www.racialequityvtnea.org/restorative-practices/

[8] Rimm-Kaufman, S. & Sandilos, L. Improving students' relationships with teachers to provide essential supports for learning. Retrieved from https://www.apa.org/education/k12/relationships

[9] DePaoli, J. L., Hernandez, L. E., Furger, R. C., & Darling-Hammond, L. (2021). *A Restorative approach for equitable education.* Learning Policy Institute. Retrieved from https://learningpolicyinstitute.org/product/wce-restorative-approach-equitable-education-brief

[10] Glossary of Education Reform (2015). Personalized learning. Retrieved from https://www.edglossary.org/personalized-learning/

[11] Merrill, S. & Gonser, S. (2021). The importance of student choice across all grade levels. Edutopia: George Lucas Foundation. Retrieved from https://www.edutopia.org/article/importance-student-choice-across-all-grade-levels

[12] Hammond, W. & Zimmerman, R. (2012). *A Strengths-Based Perspective.* Resiliency Initiatives. Retrieved from http://shed-the-light.webs.com/documents/ RSL_STRENGTH_BASED_PERSPECTIVE.pdf

Chapter 1

[1] Lopez, S. J. & Louis, M. C. (2009). The Principles of strengths-based education. *Journal of College and Character*, 10(4).

[2] Soares, A. S., Pais-Ribeiro, J. L., & Silva, I. (2019). Developmental assets predictors of life satisfaction in adolescents. *Frontiers in Psychology*, 10. https://www.frontiersin.org/article/10.3389/fpsyg.2019.00236

Harper Browne, C. (2014, September). *Youth Thrive: Advancing healthy adolescent development and well-being.* Washington, DC: Center for the Study of Social Policy.

[3] Edwards, S. & Edick, N. A. (2013). Culturally responsive teaching for significant relationships. *Journal of Praxis in Multicultural Education*, 7(1), Article 4. DOI: 10.9741/2161-2978.1058.

[4] Quaglia Institute for School Voice and Aspirations. (2016). School voice report 2016. Retrieved from quagliainstitute.org/dmsView/School_Voice_Report_2016

[5] Benner, M., Brown, C., & Jeffrey, A. (2019). Elevating student voice in education. Retrieved from https://www.americanprogress.org/issues/education-k-12/reports/2019/08/14/473197/elevating-student-voice-education/

[6] Resiliency Initiatives (2011). *Embracing a strengths-based perspective and practice in education.* Retrieved from http://www.mifras.org/know/wp-content/uploads/2017/01/Strengths-BasedSchoolCultureAndPractice.pdf

[7] Lopez, S. J. & Louis, M. C. (2009), *op. cit.*

[8] Blum, R. (2005). *School Connectedness: Improving the lives of students.* Baltimore, MD: John Hopkins Bloomberg School of Public Health.

Darling-Hammond, L., Flook, L., Cook-Harvey, C., Barron, B., & Osher, D. (2019). Implications for educational practice of the science of learning and development. *Applied Developmental Science.* https://doi.org/10.1080/10888691.2018.1537791

[9] Rimm-Kaufman, S. & Sandilos, L. (2010). Improving students' relationships with teachers to provide essential supports for learning. Retrieved from https://www.apa.org/education/k12/relationships

Sparks, S. (2019). Why teacher-student relationships matter. Retrieved from https://www.edweek.org/teaching-learning/why-teacher-student-relationships-matter/2019/03

Blum, R.W., McNeely, C.A., & Rinehart, P.M. (2002). Improving the odds: The Untapped power of schools to improve the health of teens. Center for Adolescent Health and Development, University of Minnesota, Minneapolis, MN.

Foster, C. E., Horwitz, A., Thomas, A., Opperman, K., Gipson, P., Burnside, A., Stone, D. M., & King, C. A. (2017). Connectedness to family, school, peers, and community in socially vulnerable adolescents. *Children and Youth Services Review*, 81.

[10] Blum, R. (2005), *op. cit.*

Klem A. M. & Connell J. P. (2004). Relationships matter: Linking teacher support to student engagement and achievement. *Journal of School Health,* 74(7).

[11] Mitchell, B. & Malley, J. (2003). A Pedagogy of belonging. *Online Journal of the International Child and Youth Care Network*, 50.

[12] Goodenow, C. (1993). The Psychological sense of school membership among adolescents: Scale development and educational correlates. *Psychology in the Schools.* 30(1).

[13] Borkoski, C. (2019). Cultivating belonging. *American Consortium for Equity in Education.* Retrieved from https://ace-ed.org/cultivating-belonging/

OECD (2017), PISA 2015 Results (Volume III): Students' Well-Being, PISA, OECD Publishing, Paris. http://dx.doi.org/10.1787/9789264273856-en

Osterman, K. F. (2000). Students' need for belonging in the school community. *Review of Educational Research, 70*(3). https://doi.org/10.3102/00346543070003323

Monahan, K. C., Oesterle, S. & Hawkins, J. D. (2010). Predictors and consequences of school connectedness: The Case for prevention. *The Prevention Researcher*, 17(3).

[14] Bergin, C., & Bergin, D. (2009). Attachment in the classroom. *Educational Psychology Review, 21*

Riley, H. & Terada, Y. (2019). Bringing the science of learning into classrooms. Edutopia: George Lucas Foundation. Retrieved from https://www.edutopia.org/article/bringing-science-learning-classrooms

Blum, R. W. (2005) A Case for school connectedness. *Educational Leadership*, 62(7).

Blum, R. (2005), *op. cit.*

[15] Blum, R. (2005), *op. cit.*

Wingspread declaration on school connections. (2004). *Journal of School Health*, 74(7).

[16] Dusenbury, L. (2020). Creating a safe classroom environment. Retrieved from https://www.educationworld.com/a_curr/creating-safe-classroom-environment-climate.shtml

[17] Powell, W. & Kusuma-Powell, O. (2011). *How to teach now: Five keys to personalized learning in the global classroom.* Alexandria, VA: ASCD.

[18] Darling-Hammond, L., Flook, L., Cook-Harvey, C., Barron, B., & Osher, D. (2019). Implications for educational practice of the science of learning and development. *Applied Developmental Science.* https://doi.org/10.1080/10888691.2018.1537791.

[19] Vargas, B. C. & Steele, D. (2015). Creating an identity-safe classroom. Edutopia: George Lucas Foundation. Retrieved from https://www.edutopia.org/blog/creating-an-identity-safe-classroom-becki-cohn-vargas-dorothy-steele

[20] Hammond, Z. (2015). 3 Tips to make any lesson more culturally responsive. Retrieved from https://www.cultofpedagogy.com/culturally-responsive-teaching-strategies/

[21] Hammond, Z. (2015), *op. cit.*

[22] Deans for Impact (2015). The Science of learning. Retrieved from http://www.deansforimpact.org/wp-content/uploads/2016/12/The_Science_of_Learning.pdf

[23] Lynch, M. (2012). What is culturally responsive pedagogy? *Huffington Post.* Retrieved from http://www.huffingtonpost.com/matthew-lynch-edd/culturally-responsivepedagogy_b_1147364.html

Kozleski, E. B. (2000). *Culturally responsive teaching matters!* Equity Alliance. Retrieved from http://guide.swiftschools.org/sites/default/files/ documents/CulturallyResponsiveTeaching-Matters.pdf

[24] González, N., Moll, L.C., & Amanti, C.. (2005). *Funds of knowledge: Theorizing practices in households, communities, and classrooms.* Mahwah, NJ: Lawrence Erlbaum Associates.

Vélez-Ibáñez, C.G., & Greenberg, J.B. (1992). Formation and transformation of funds of knowledge among U.S. Mexican households. *Anthropology & Education Quarterly,* 23(4).

[25] Rucker, N. W. (2019) Getting started with culturally responsive teaching. Edutopia: George Lucas Foundation. Retrieved from https://www.edutopia.org/article/getting-started-culturally-responsive-teaching

Krasnoff, B. (2016). *Culturally responsive teaching: A Guide to evidence-based practices for teaching all students equitably.* Retrieved from https://education-northwest.org/sites/default/files/resources/culturally-responsive-teaching.pdf

Gay, G. (2010). *Culturally responsive teaching: Theory, research, and practice, 2nd edition.* New York, NY: Teachers College Press.

[26] Kimble, A. (2020). A Teacher's journey toward culturally relevant teaching practices. Retrieved from https://xqsuperschool.org/rethinktogether/culturally-relevant-teaching-practices/

[27] Krasnoff, B. (2016), *op. cit.*

Breiseth, l., Garcia, S., & Butler, S. (2014-2021). What is culturally responsive teaching? Retrieved from https://www.understood.org/articles/en/what-is-culturally-responsive-teaching

[28] Ferlazzo, L. (2020). Steps to make classrooms more culturally responsive. Education Week. Retrieved from https://www.edweek.org/teaching-learning/opinion-steps-to-make-classrooms-more-culturally-responsive/2020/03

Regional Educational Laboratory at Mathematica. (2019). *Teaching diverse learners using culturally responsive pedagogy* [Fact sheet]. https://ies.ed.gov/ncee/edlabs/regions/midatlantic/app/Docs/Infographics/RELMA_Culturally_responsive_pedagogy_fact_sheet.pdf

[29] Breiseth, L., Garcia, S., & Butler, S. (2014-2021), *op. cit.*

[30] Diller, J.V. & Moule, J. (2005). Cultural competence: A primer for educators. Belmont, CA: Thomas Wadsworth.

[31] Ladson-Billings, G. (2009). *The Dreamkeepers: Successful teachers of African American children*, 2nd edition. San Francisco, CA: Jossey-Bass.

Klotz, M. B. (2006). Culturally competent schools: Guidelines for secondary school principals. *National Association of School Psychologist Journal*, 6.

[32] Diller, J.V. & Moule, J. (2005), *op. cit.*

[33] Darling-Hammond, L., & Cook-Harvey, C. M. (2018). *Educating the whole child: Improving school climate to support student success.* Palo Alto, CA: Learning Policy Institute.

[34] Khan, S. (2021). Cultural humility vs. cultural competence— And Why providers need both. Retrieved from https://www.bmcortho.com/healthcity/policy-and-industry/cultural-humility-vs-cultural-competence-providers-need-both

Nelson, A. (2021). Why cultural humility is key to successful employee benefits. Retrieved from https://www.benefitspro.com/2021/01/29/why-cultural-humility-is-key-to-successful-employee-benefits/?slreturn=20210829210445

TED. (2017, December 1). *Cultural Humility|Juliana Mosley* [Video]. YouTube https://www.youtube.com/watch?v=Ww_ml21L7Ns

[35] Waters, A. & Asbill, L. (2013). Reflections on cultural humility. Retrieved from https://www.apa.org/pi/families/resources/newsletter/2013/08/cultural-humility

[36] Tervalon, M., & Murray-García, J. (1998). Cultural humility versus cultural competence: A Critical distinction in defining physician training outcomes in multicultural education. *Journal of Health Care for the Poor and Underserved*, 9(2). https://doi.org/10.1353/hpu.2010.0233.

[37] Haynes-Mendez, K. & Engelsmeier, J. (2020) Cultivating cultural humility in education. *Childhood Education*, 96(3). DOI: 10.1080/00094056.2020.1766656

Foronda, C. (2020). A Theory of cultural humility. *Journal of Transcultural Nursing, 31*(1). https://doi.org/10.1177/1043659619875184.

[38] Learning for Justice - formerly Teaching Tolerance (2018). Critical practices for anti-bias education. Retrieved from https://www.learningforjustice.org/sites/default/files/2021-11/LFJ-2111-Critical-Practices-for-Anti-bias-Ed-November-2021-11172021.pdf

[39] Isaacson, M. (2014). Clarifying concepts: Cultural humility or competency. *Journal of Professional Nursing*, 30.

Murray-Garcia, J., & Tervalon, M. (2014). The concept of cultural humility. *Health Affairs*, 33(7).

[40] TED. (2017, December 1). *Cultural Humility|Juliana Mosley* [Video], *op. cit.*

[41] Waters, A. & Asbill, L. (2013), *op. cit.*

[42] Khan, S. (2021), *op. cit.*

[43] Rychly, L., & Graves, E. (2012). Teacher characteristics for culturally responsive pedagogy. *Multicultural Perspectives*, 14(1). https://doi.org/10.1080/15210960.2012.646853

[44] Galinsky, A. D., & Ku, G. (2004). The Effects of perspective-taking on prejudice: The Moderating role of self-evaluation. *Personality and Social Psychology Bulletin*, 30.

Vescio, T. K., Sechrist, G. B., & Paolucci, M. P. (2003). Perspective taking and prejudice reduction: The Mediational role of empathy arousal and situational attributions. *European Journal of Social Psychology*, 33.

[45] Sparks, S. D. (2019) Why teacher-student relationships matter. Education Week. Retrieved from https://www.edweek.org/teaching-learning/why-teacher-student-relationships-matter/2019/03

[46] Cooper, B. (2004). Empathy, interaction and caring: Teachers' roles in a constrained environment. *Pastoral Care in Education*, 22(3). https://doi.org/10.1111/j.0264-3944.2004.00299.x.

[47] Galinsky, A. D., Ku, G., & Wang, C. S. (2005). Perspective-taking and self-other overlap: Fostering social bonds and facilitating social coordination. *Group Processes & Intergroup Relations*, 8(2). https://doi.org/10.1177/1368430205051060.

[48] Abacioglu, C. S., Volman, M., & Fischer, A. H. (2019). Teacher's multicultural attitudes and perspective taking abilities as factors in culturally responsive teaching. *British Journal of Educational Psychology*, 90.

McAllister, G., & Irvine, J. J. (2002). The Role of empathy in teaching culturally diverse students: A Qualitative study of teachers' beliefs. *Journal of Teacher Education*, 53. https://doi.org/10.1177/002248702237397.

Chapter 2

[1] Zimmerman, B. J. & Schunk, D. H. (Eds.) (2009). *Self-regulated learning and academic achievement: Theoretical perspectives*, 2nd edition. New York: Routledge.

[2] Mattern, K., Burrus, J., Camara, W., O'Connor, R., Hansen, M. A., Gambrell, J., Casillas, A., and Bobek, B. (2014). Broadening the Definition of College and Career Readiness: A Holistic Approach. ACT Research Report Series. Retrieved from http://files.eric.ed.gov/fulltext/ED555591.pdf

[3] Zimmerman, B. J. (2002). Becoming a self-regulated learner: An Overview. *Theory Into Practice*, 41(2). Zimmerman, B. J. (1990). Self-regulated learning and academic achievement: An Overview. *Educational Psychologist*, 25(1).

[4] National Academies of Sciences, Engineering, and Medicine (2018). *How people learn II: Learners, contexts, and cultures.* Washington, DC: The National Academies Press. https://doi.org/10.17226/24783.

[5] Hattie, J. A. C. & Donoghue, G. M. (2016). Learning strategies: A Synthesis and conceptual model. *NPJ Science of Learning*, 1(16013). https://doi.org/10.1038/npjscilearn.2016.13.

[6] Toro, S. (2021). How to guide students to self-regulated learning. Edutopia: George Lucas Educational Foundation. Retrieved from https://www.edutopia.org/article/how-guide-students-self-regulated-learning

[7] Zimmerman, B. J. (1989). A social cognitive view of self-regulated academic learning. *Journal of Educational Psychology*, 81(3).

Zimmerman, B. J. (1990). Self-regulated academic learning and achievement: The Emergence of a social cognitive perspective. *Educational Psychology Review*, 2(2).

[8] Loyens, S. M. M., Magda, J. & Rikers, R. M. J. P. (2008). Self-directed learning in problem-based learning and its relationships with self-regulated learning. *Educational Psychology Review*, 20(4). https://doi.org/10.1007/s10648-008-9082-7.

Zimmerman, B. J. (2002). Achieving self-regulation: The Trial and triumph of adolescence. In F. Pajares and T. Urdan (Eds.), *Academic motivation of adolescents*. Greenwich, Ct.: Information Age Publishing.

[9] Ferlazzo, L. (2017). Response: Student goal-setting in the classroom. Education Week. Retrieved from https://www.edweek.org/teaching-learning/opinion-response-student-goal-setting-in-the-classroom/2017/01

[10] Willis, J. (2011). Whose children will get the best jobs in the 21st century? *Psychology Today*. Retrieved from https://www.psychologytoday.com/blog/radical-teaching/201104/whose-children-will-get-the-best-jobs-in-the-21st-century

Wolters, C. A. (2010). *Self-Regulated Learning and the 21st Century Competencies*.

[11] Covington, M. V. (2000). Goal theory, motivation, and school achievement: An Integrative review. *Annual Review of Psychology*, 51.

[12] Dweck, C. S. (1986). Motivational processes affecting learning. *American Psychologist*, 41(10).

[13] McTighe, J. & O'Connor, K. (2005). Seven practices for effective learning. *Educational Leadership*, 63(3).

[14] Wiggins, G. (2012). Seven keys to effective feedback. *Educational Leadership*, 70(1).

[15] Gibbs, G. & Simpson, C. (2004). Conditions under which assessment supports students' learning. *Learning and Teaching in Higher Education*, 1.

[16] Wiggins, G. (2012), *op. cit.*

[17] Lopez, S. J. & Louis, M. C. (2009). The Principles of strengths-based education. *Journal of College and Character*, 10(4).

[18] Frey, N., Fisher, D., & Smith, D. (2019). *All learning is social and emotional: Helping students develop essential skills for the classroom and beyond*. Alexandra, VA: ASCD.

[19] Stenger, M. (2014). 5 Research-based tips for providing students with meaningful feedback. Edutopia: George Lucas Foundation. Retrieved from https://www.edutopia.org/blog/tips-providing-studentsmeaningful-feedback-marianne-stenger

[20] ADHD (2019). What does metacognition have to do with executive functions? Retrieved from https://orchidadhd.com/2019/05/10/what-does-metacognition-have-to-do-with-executive-functions/

[21] McTighe, J. (2016). How should we teach toward success with performance tasks? (Part 7). Retrieved from https://blog.performancetask.com/how-should-we-teach-toward-success-with-performance-tasks-part-7-93f2279b625

[22] Cooper, R. (2017). How can educators best promote student agency? Retrieved from https://www.k12dive.com/news/how-can-educators-best-promote-student-agency/508050/

²³ Norwood, A. (n.d.). What does self-assessment and self-reflection bring to the learning journey? Retrieved from https://schoolbox.com.au/blog/what-does-self-assessment-and-self-reflection-bring-to-the-learning-journey?

²⁴ ADHD (2019), *op. cit.*

²⁵ Center on the Developing Child, Harvard University (2015). *Enhancing and practicing executive function skills with children from infancy to adolescence.* Retrieved from http://www.developingchild.harvard.edu.

²⁶ Center on the Developing Child, Harvard University (2011). *Building the brain's "air traffic control" system: How early experiences shape the development of executive function* (*Working Paper No. 11*). Retrieved from http://www.developingchild.harvard.edu

²⁷ Lawson, G. M., Hook, C. J., Hackman, D. A., & Farah, M. J. (2015). Socioeconomic status and neurocognitive development: Executive functions. In J. A. Griffin, P. McCardle, and L. Freund (Eds.), *Executive function in preschool-age children: Integrating measurement, neurodevelopment, and translational research.* Washington, D.C.: American Psychological Association Press.

Goldstein, S., Naglieri, J. A., Princiotta, D., & Otero, T. M. (2014). Introduction: A History of executive functioning as a theoretical and clinical construct. In S. Goldstein and J. A. Naglieri (Eds.), *Handbook of Executive Functioning*. New York: Springer.

²⁸ Wilson, D. (2015). Strategies for strengthening the brain's executive functions. Edutopia: George Lucas Education Foundation. Retrieved from http://www.edutopia.org/blog/strategies-strengthening-brains-executive-functions-donna-wilson-marcus-conyers

²⁹ Willis, J. (2011), *op. cit.*

³⁰ Donker, A. S., de Boer, H., Kostons, D., van Ewijk, C. D., & van der Werf, M. P. (2014). Effectiveness of learning strategy instruction on academic performance: A Meta-analysis. *Educational Research Review*, 11.

Ohtani, K. & Hisasaka, T. (2018). Beyond intelligence: A Meta-analytic review of the relationship among metacognition, intelligence, and academic performance. *Metacognition and Learning*, 13.

Winne, P. H. & Perry, N. E. (2000). Measuring self-regulated learning. In the M. Boekaerts, P. R. Pintrich, and M. Zeidner (Eds.), *Handbook of self-regulation*. Orlando, FL: Academic Press.

[31] National Research Council (2012). *Education for life and work: Developing transferable knowledge and skills in the 21st century.* The National Academies Press. https://doi.org/10.17226/1339

Beach, P. T., Anderson, R. C., Jacovidis, J. N., & Chadwick, K. L. (2020). *Making the abstract explicit: The Role of metacognition in teaching and learning.* Inflexion Policy Paper: Metacognition in Education. Retrieved from https://www.ibo.org/globalassets/publications/ib-research/policy/metacognition-policy-paper.pdf

[32] Beach, P. T., Anderson, R. C., Jacovidis, J. N., & Chadwick, K. L. (2020), *op. cit.*

Fadel, C., Trilling, B., & Bialik, M. (2015). Metacognition—Reflecting on learning goals, strategies, and results. In *Four-dimensional education: The Competencies learners need to succeed.* Center for Curriculum Design.

[33] TEAL Center Staff (2010). *Metacognitive processes* [TEAL Center Fact Sheet No. 4]. LINCS. Retrieved from https://lincs.ed.gov/state-resources/federal-initiatives/teal/guide/metacognitive

[34] Fadel, C., Trilling, B., & Bialik, M. (2015). Metacognition—Reflecting on learning goals, strategies, and results. In *Four-dimensional education: The Competencies learners need to succeed.* Center for Curriculum Design.

[35] Perry, N. E., Hutchinson, L., & Thauberger, C. (2008). Talking about teaching self-regulated learning: Scaffolding student teachers' development and use of practices that promote self-regulated learning. *International Journal of Educational Research*, 47(2).

[36] Stanton, J. D., Sebesta, A. J., & Dunlosky, J. (2021). Fostering metacognition to support student learning and performance. *CBE-Life Science and Education*, 20(2).

[37] TEAL Center Staff (2010), *op. cit.*

[38] Donovan, S. M., Bransford, J. D., & Pellegrino, J. W. (1999). *How people learn: Bridging research and practice.* Washington, DC: National Academy Press. TEAL Center Staff (2010), *op. cit.*

[39] Beach, P. T., Anderson, R. C., Jacovidis, J. N., & Chadwick, K. L. (2020), *op. cit.*

[40] National Research Council (2012), *op. cit.*

[41] Donovan, S. M., Bransford, J. D., & Pellegrino, J. W. (1999), *op. cit.*

[42] Roebers, C. M. (2017). Executive function and metacognition: Towards a unifying framework of cognitive self-regulation. *Developmental Review*, 45.

[43] Meltzer, L., Pollica, L. S., & Barzillai, M. (2007). Executive function in the classroom. In L. Meltzer, Ed. *Executive function in education: From theory to practice*. New York: The Guilford Press.

[44] American Institutes for Research (2018). Key findings and implications of the science of learning and development. Retrieved from https://turnaroundusa.org/wp-content/uploads/2018/02/Key-Findings-and-Implications-of-the-Science-of-Learning-Development.pdf

Chapter 3

[1] Gardner, H. (1991). *The Unschooled mind: How children think and how schools should teach*. New York: Basic Books.

[2] Gardner, H. (1983). *Frames of mind: The Theory of multiple intelligences*. New York: Basic Books.

Gardner, H. (1999). *Intelligence reframed: Multiple intelligences for the 21st century*. New York: Basic Books.

[3] Edutopia (2009). Big thinkers: Howard Gardner on multiple intelligences. Retrieved from https://www.edutopia.org/multiple-intelligences-howard-gardner-video

[4] Voice. (2014). In S. Abbott (Ed.), The glossary of education reform. Retrieved from edglossary.org/voice

[5] Benner, M., Brown, C., & Jeffrey, A. (2019). Elevating student voice in education. Retrieved from https://www.americanprogress.org/issues/education-k-12/reports/2019/08/14/473197/elevating-student-voice-education/

[6] Armstrong, T. (2018). 8 Ways to boost student engagement by giving students choices. Retrieved from https://www.institute4learning.com/2018/05/04/8-ways-to-boost-student-engagement-by-giving-students-choices/

[7] Armstrong, T. (2018). *Multiple intelligences in the classroom, 4th edition*. Alexandria, VA: ASCD.

[8] Gardner, H. (1983), *op. cit*.

[9] Campbell, L. (1997). Variations on a theme—How teachers interpret MI theory. *Educational Leadership* 55(1).

[10] Moran, S. & Gardner, H. (2007). 'Hill, skill, and will': Executive function from a multiple-intelligences perspective. In L. Melter (Ed.), *Executive function in education: From theory to practice*. New York: The Guilford Press.

[11] Center on the Developing Child, Harvard University (2015). *Enhancing and practicing executive function skills with children from infancy to adolescence.* Retrieved from http://www.developingchild.harvard.edu

[12] Carney, R. N. & Levin, J. R. (2002). Pictorial illustrations still improve students' learning from text. *Educational Psychology Review*, 14. https://doi.org/10.1023/A:1013176309260

Bui, D. C. & McDaniel, M. A. (2015). Enhancing learning during lecture note-taking using outlines and illustrative diagrams. *Journal of Applied Research in Memory and Cognition*, 4(2).

[13] Gardner, H. (2011). Multiple intelligences: The First thirty years. Retrieved from https://howardgardner01.files.wordpress.com/2012/06/intro-frames-of-mind_30-years.pdf

[14] Gardner, H. (2013). *Frequently Asked Questions—Multiple Intelligences and Related Educational Topics.* Retrieved from http://multipleintelligencesoasis.org/wp-content/uploads/2013/06/faq.pdf

[15] Armstrong, T. (2009). *Multiple intelligences in the classroom, 3rd edition.* Alexandria, VA: ASCD.

[16] Armstrong, T. (2018), *op. cit.*

[17] Darling-Hammond, L., Austin, K., Lit, I., Martin, D., & Gardner, H. (2003). Different kinds of smart: Multiple intelligences. Session 4 of The Learning Classroom: Theory Into Practice. Annenberg Learner. Retrieved from https://www.learner.org/courses/learningclassroom/support/04_mult_intel.pdf

[18] Brownlee, K., Rawana, E. P. & MacArthur, J. (2012). Implementation of a strengths-based approach to teaching in an elementary school. *Journal of Teaching and Learning*, 8(1).

[19] More information regarding the MIDAS™ can be found at www.miresearch.org/midas/midas-2/ Shearer also maintains a list of schools and organizations that use the assessment at www.miresearch.org/midas/midas-2/schools-universities-organizations/

[20] Gardner, H. (2013), *op. cit.*

[21] Gardner, H. (1999), *op. cit.*

Gardner, H. (2013), *op. cit.*

[22] Lopez, S. J. & Louis, M. C. (2009). The Principles of strengths-based education. *Journal of College and Character*, 10(4).

[23] Darling-Hammond, L., Austin, K., Lit, I., Martin, D., & Gardner, H. (2003), *op. cit.*

[24] Anderson, E. C. (2004). *What is strengths-based education?: A tentative answer by someone who strives to be a strengths-based educator.* Unpublished manuscript. Retrieved from https://www.weber.edu/WSUImages/leadership/docs/sq/strengths-base-ed.pdf

[25] Darling-Hammond, L., Austin, K., Lit, I., Martin, D., & Gardner, H. (2003), *op. cit.*

[26] Armstrong, T. (2018), *op. cit.*

[27] Kornhaber, M., Fierros, E., and Veenema, S. (2004). *Multiple Intelligences: Best Ideas from Research and Practice.* Boston: Allyn & Bacon.

[28] Armstrong, T. (2018), *op. cit.*

[29] Gardner, H. (1993), *op. cit.*

[30] Darling-Hammond, L., Austin, K., Lit, I., Martin, D., & Gardner, H. (2003), *op. cit.*

[31] Lopez, S. J. & Louis, M. C. (2009), *op. cit.*

[32] Green, C. & Harrington, C. (2020). How implementing voice & choice can improve student engagement. Retrieved from https://michiganvirtual.org/blog/how-implementing-voice-choice-can-improve-student-engagement/

[33] Darling-Hammond, L. (2010). Performance counts: Assessment systems that support high-quality learning. Council of Chief State School Officers. Retrieved from https://edpolicy.stanford.edu/sites/default/files/publications/performance-counts-assessment-systems-support-high-quality-learning.pdf

[34] Armstrong, T. (2018), *op. cit.*

Chapter 4

[1] Waxman, H. C., Gray, J. P., & Padron, Y. N. (2003). *Review of research on educational resilience.* Center for Research on Education, Diversity & Excellence. Retrieved from https://escholarship.org/content/qt7x695885/qt7x695885.pdf

[2] Horowitz, J. M. & Graf, N. (2019). Most U.S. teens see anxiety and depression as a major problem among their peers. Pew Research Center. Retrieved from https://www.pewresearch.org/social-trends/2019/02/20/most-u-s-teens-see-anxiety-and-depression-as-a-major-problem-among-their-peers/

Twenge, J. M., Cooper, A. B., Joiner, T. E., Duffy, M. E., & Binau, S. G. (2019). Age, period, and cohort trends in mood disorder indicators and suicide-related outcomes in a nationally representative dataset, 2005-2017). *Journal of Abnormal Psychology*, 128(3).

Centers for Disease Control and Prevention. Facts about suicide. Retrieved from https://www.cdc.gov/suicide/facts/index.html

[3] Calderon, V. J. (2020). U.S. parents say COVID-19 harming child's mental health. GALLUP. Retrieved from https://news.gallup.com/poll/312605/parents-say-covid-harming-child-mental-health.aspx

Racine, N., McArthur, B. A., Cooke, J. E., Eirich, R., Zhu, J. & Madigan, S. (2021). Global prevalence of depressive and anxiety symptoms in children and adolescents during COVID-19: A Meta-analysis. *Jama Pediatrics*, 175(11).

Hill, R. M., Rufino, K., Kurian, S., Saxena, J., Saxena, K., & Williams, L. (2021). Suicide ideation and attempts in a pediatric emergency department before and during COVID-19. *Pediatrics*, 147(3).

Choi, J. (2021). Las Vegas-area district moves to partially reopen schools amid surge in student suicides. The Hill. Retrieved from https://thehill.com/homenews/state-watch/535598-las-vegas-to-push-reopening-schools-amid-surge-in-student-suicides.

[4] Hammond, W. & Zimmerman, R. (2012). A Strengths-Based perspective. Resiliency Initiatives. Retrieved from http://shed-the-light.webs.com/documents/ RSL_STRENGTH_BASED_PERSPECTIVE.pdf

[5] Bromley, E., Johnson, J. G., & Cohen, P. (2006). Personality strengths in adolescence and decreased risk of developing mental health problems in early adulthood. *Comprehensive Psychiatry*, 47(4).

Epstein, M. H., Hertzog, M. A., & Reid, R. (2001). The Behavioral and emotional rating scale: Long term test–retest reliability. *Behavioral Disorders*, 26(4).

[6] Gable, S. L. & Haidt, J. (2005). What (and why) is positive psychology? *Review of General Psychology*, 9(2).

[7] Durlak, J. A., Domitrovich, C. E., Weissberg, R. P., & Gullotta, T. P., (Eds.) (2015). *Handbook of social and emotional learning: Research and practice*. New York: The Guilford Press.

[8] Lopez, S. J. (2013). *Making hope happen: Create the future you want for yourself and others*. New York: Simon & Schuster.

[9] Day, L., Hanson, K., Maltby, J., Proctor, C., & Wood A. (2010). Hope uniquely predicts objective academic achievement above intelligence, personality, and previous academic achievement. *Journal of Research in Personality*, 44(4).

[10] Lopez, S. J., Rose, S., Robinson, C., Marques, S. C., & Pais-Ribeiro, J. (2014). Measuring and promoting hope in schoolchildren. In M. J. Furlong, R. Gilman, and E. S. Huebner (Eds.), *Handbook of positive psychology in schools, 2nd edition*. New York: Taylor & Francis.

[11] Snyder, C. R. (1994). *The Psychology of hope: You can get there from here*. New York: The Free Press.

Lopez (2013), *op. cit.*

[12] Lopez et al. (2014), *op. cit.*

[13] Snyder, C. R., Shorey, H. S., Cheavens, J., Pulvers, K. M., Adams, V. H., III, & Wiklund, C. (2002). Hope and academic success in college. *Journal of Educational Psychology*, 94(4).

[14] Snyder, C. R., Feldman, D. B., Shorey, H. S., & Rand, K. L. (2002). Hopeful choices: A School counselor's guide to hope theory. *Professional School Counseling*, 5(5).

[15] Usher, A. & Kober, N. (2012). *Can goals motivate students?* Center on Education Policy, The George Washington University Graduate School of Education and Human Development. Retrieved from https://archive.org/stream/ERIC_ED532668/ERIC_ED532668_djvu.txt

[16] Marques, S. C. & Lopez, S. J. (2011). Building hope in our children. *Communiqué of the National Association of School Psychologists*, 40(3).

[17] McKnight, P. E. & Kashdan, T. B. (2009). Purpose in life as a system that creates and sustains health and well-being: An Integrative, testable theory. *Review of General Psychology*, 13(3).

[18] Paunesku, D., Walton, G. M., Romero, C., Smith, E. N., Yeager, D. S., & Dweck C. S. (2015). Mind-set interventions are a scalable treatment for academic underachievement. *Psychological Science*, 26(6).

[19] Farrington, C.A., Roderick, M., Allensworth, E., Nagaoka, J., Keyes, T.S., Johnson, D.W., & Beechum, N.O. (2012). *Teaching adolescents to become learners. The Role of noncognitive factors in shaping school performance: A Critical literature review*. Chicago: University of Chicago Consortium on Chicago School Research.

[20] Usher, A. & Kober, N. (2012), *op. cit.*

[21] Dweck, C. S., Walton, G. M., & Cohen, G. L. (2014). *Academic tenacity: Mindsets and skills that promote long-term learning.* Bill and Melinda Gates Foundation. Retrieved from https://ed.stanford.edu/sites/default/files/manual/dweck-walton-cohen-2014.pdf

[22] Walker, D. & Darling, S. K. (2009). Resiliency—Why it matters. In *Closing the poverty and culture gap: Strategies to reach every student.* Thousand Oaks, Ca.: Corwin Publishers.

[23] Barr, R. D. & Parrett, W. H. (2007). Engage parents, communities, and schools to work as partners. In *The Kids left behind: Catching up the underachieving children of poverty.* Bloomington, Ind.: Solution Tree.

Service learning (2017). National Dropout Prevention Center/Network at Clemson University. Retrieved from http://dropoutprevention.org/effective-strategies/ser.

[24] Brail, S. (2016). Quantifying the value of service-learning: A Comparison of grade achievement between service-learning and non-service-learning students. *International Journal of Teaching and Learning in Higher Education,* 28(2). Astin, A. W., Vogelgesang, L. J., Ikeda, E. K., & Yee, J. A. (2000). How service learning affects students. *Higher Education.* Paper 144.

[25] Melter, L. (Ed.) (2007). *Executive function in education: From theory to practice.* New York: The Guilford Press.

[26] Ayduk, O., Mendoza-Denton, R., Mischel, W., Downey, G., Peake, P. K., & Rodriguez, M. (2000). Regulating the interpersonal self: strategic self-regulation for coping with rejection sensitivity. *Journal of personality and social psychology,* 79(5).

Duckworth, A.L., Peterson, C., Matthews, M.D., & Kelly, D.R. (2007) Grit: Perseverance and passion for long-term goals. *Journal of Personality and Social Psychology,* 92.

[27] Heshmat, S. (2016). How self-control can help you live a healthier life. *Psychology Today.* Retrieved from https://www.psychologytoday.com/us/blog/science-choice/201607/how-self-control-can-help-you-live-healthier-life.

Tangney, J. P., Baumeister, R. F., & Boone, A. L. (2004). High self-control predicts good adjustment, less pathology, better grades, and interpersonal success. *Journal of personality,* 72(2). https://doi.org/10.1111/j.0022-3506.2004.00263.x.

[28] Mischel, W., Ayduk, O., Berman, M. G., Casey, B. J., Gotlib, I. H., Jonides, J., & Shoda, Y. (2010). 'Willpower' over the life span: decomposing self-regula-

tion. *Social Cognitive and Affective Neuroscience.* doi:10.1093/scan/nsq081.

[29] Duckworth, A. L. & Seligman, M. E. P. (2005). Self-discipline outdoes IQ in predicting academic performance of adolescents. *Psychological Science, 16.*

[30] Tangney, J. P., Baumeister, R. F., & Boone, A. L. (2004), *op. cit.*

[31] Duckworth, A. L. (2011). The significance of self-control. *Proceedings of the National Academy of Science* (PNAS), 108(7).

[32] Moffitt, T. E., Arseneault, L., Belsky, D., Dickson, N., Hancox, R. J., Harrington, H., Houts, R., Poulton, R., Roberts, B. W., Ross, S., Sears, m. R., Thomson, W. M., & Caspi, A. (2011). A gradient of childhood self-control predicts health, wealth, and public safety. *Proceedings of the National Academy of Science* (PNAS), 108(7).

[33] Parrish, N. (2018). How to teach self-regulation. Edutopia: George Lucas Foundation. Retrieved from https://www.edutopia.org/article/how-teach-self-regulation

[34] Doran, G. T. (1981). There's a S.M.A.R.T. way to write management's goals and objectives. *Management Review* (AMA FORUM), 70(11).

[35] Edutopia (2019). Developing executive function with priority lists. George Lucas Foundation. Retrieved from https://www.edutopia.org/video/developing-executive-function-priority-lists

[36] Fein, A. M. (2021). Guiding students to improve executive functioning skills. Edutopia: George Lucas Foundation. Retrieved from https://www.edutopia.org/article/guiding-students-improve-executive-functioning-skills

[37] Edutopia (2019). Teaching self-regulation by modeling. George Lucas Foundation. Retrieved from https://www.edutopia.org/video/teaching-self-regulation-modeling

Chapter 5

[1] Schleifer, D., Rinehart, C., & Yanisch, T. (2017). Teacher collaboration in perspective: A guide to research. Spencer Foundation and Public Agenda. Retrieved from https://files.eric.ed.gov/fulltext/ED591332.pdf

[2] Caskey, M. M. & Carpenter, J. (2014). Building teacher collaboration schoolwide. *Association for Middle Level Education (AMLE) Magazine.*

[3] DuFour, R. (2004). What is a "professional learning community"? Retrieved from https://www.ascd.org/el/articles/what-is-a-professional-learning-community.

[4] Ferlazzo, L. (2021). 'A professional learning community is not a faculty, grade level, or department meeting.' Education Week. Retrieved from https://www.edweek.org/leadership/opinion-a-professional-learning-community-is-not-a-faculty-grade-level-or-department-meeting/2021/04

Miller, A. (2020). Creating effective professional learning communities. Retrieved from https://www.edutopia.org/article/creating-effective-professional-learning-communities

[5] Creating strengths-based classrooms and schools: A Practice guide for classrooms and schools. (2013). Retrieved from https://albertamentors.ca/wp-content/uploads/2013/10/SB_for_Schools_and_Classrooms.pdf.

[6] Darling-Hammond, L., Hyler, M. E., & Gardner, M. (2017). *Effective Teacher Professional Development*. Palo Alto, CA: Learning Policy Institute. https://doi.org/10.54300/122.311.

EdVestors and Rennie Center for Education Research & Policy (2014). *Making space: The Value of teacher collaboration*. Retrieved from https://www.edvestors.org/wp-content/uploads/2016/05/EdVestors-Making-Space-The-Value-of-Teacher-Collaboration-2014.pdf

[7] EdVestors and Rennie Center for Education Research & Policy (2014), *op. cit.*

[8] Johnson, S.M., Reinhorn, S. K., & Simon, N. S. (2018). Ending isolation: The Payoff of teacher teams in successful high-poverty urban schools. *Teachers College Record*, 120.

[9] Brownell, M.T., Yeager, E. Rennells, M.S. & Riley, T. (1997). Teachers working together: What learning educators and researchers should know. *Teacher Education and Special Education*, 20.

[10] Caskey, M. M. & Carpenter, J. (2014). Building teacher collaboration schoolwide. *Association for Middle Level Education (AMLE) Magazine*.

[11] Caskey, M. M. & Carpenter, J. (2014), *op. cit.*

[12] Vangrieken, K., Dochy, F., Raes, E., & Kyndt, E. (2015). Teacher collaboration: A systematic review. *Educational Research Review*, 15.

[13] Huseman, R. C. (2012). *Relational intelligence: The new smart*. Florida: Equity Press.

[14] Gagne, Y. (2019 November 4). Esther Perel's new podcast is about the relationships we have at work. Retrieved from https://www.fastcompany.com/90419232/esther-perels-new-podcast-is-about-the-relationships-we-have-at-work

Huseman, R. C. (2012), *op. cit.*

[15] Gagne, Y. (2019 November 4), *op. cit.*

[16] Huseman, R. C. (2012), *op. cit.*

Pless, N. M. & Maak, T. (2005), *op. cit.* Relational intelligence for leading responsibly in a connected world. https://doi.org/10.5465/ambpp.2005.18783524.

[17] Huseman, R. C. (2012), *op. cit.*

[18] Huseman, R. C. (2012), *op. cit.*

Pless, N. M. & Maak, T. (2005). Relational intelligence for leading responsibly in a connected world. https://doi.org/10.5465/ambpp.2005.18783524.

[19] Mayer, J. D. Roberts, R. D. & Barsade, D. G. (2008). Human abilities: Emotional intelligence. *Annual Review of Psychology*, 59(1).

[20] Five to Nine (2020). On building relational intelligence. Retrieved from https://medium.com/@info_37650/on-building-relational-intelligence-28faf1dbaf01

[21] Officevibe Content Team (2021). How to build great relationships at work with relational intelligence. Retrieved from https://officevibe.com/blog/building-relational-intelligence

[22] Lencioni, P. (2002). *The five dysfunctions of a team: A leadership fable*. San Francisco, CA: Jossey-Bass

[23] Covey, S. (2006). *The Speed of trust: The One thing that changes everything*. New York: Free Press.

[24] Lencioni, P. (2002), *op. cit.*

[25] St-Aubin, N. (2021). How to build team trust and boost collaboration: 5 Strategies. Retrieved from https://officevibe.com/blog/build-team-trust

[26] Swartz, M. I., Bartlett, J. D., & Vele-Tabaddor, E. (2016). Strengths-based education and practices. In The SAGE *Encyclopedia of Contemporary Early Childhood Education*. Thousand Oaks: SAGE Publications, Inc.

[27] Bronson, M. H. & Merki, D. (2005). Skills for healthy relationships. *Glencoe Health*. New York: Glencoe/McGraw-Hill. https://oldsite.slusd.us/old-website/SLUSD-DO/www.sanleandro.k12.ca.us/cms/lib/CA01001252/Centricity/Domain/868/chap10.pdf

[28] Batton, J., Jones, T. S., Cuervo, A., Bazron, B. J., & Gorin, D. (2006). Managing and resolving conflicts effectively in schools and classrooms. U. S. Department of Education's Safe and Drug Free Schools Office. Retrieved from https://www.creducation.net/resources/resolving_conflicts/

²⁹ Team MyHub (2021). Collaborative communication: Why it matters. Retrieved from https://www.myhubintranet.com/collaborative-communication/

³⁰ Digital Workplace (2021). How to inspire communication and collaboration in 2021. Retrieved from https://kissflow.com/digital-workplace/collaboration/how-to-inspire-communication-and-collaboration/

³¹ Five to Nine (2020), *op. cit.*

³² Aiello, C. G. (2021). 7 Ways to create relational intelligence for remote leaders. Retrieved from https://inside.6q.io/relational-intelligence-for-remote-leaders/

³³ Team MyHub (2021). Collaborative communication: Why it matters. Retrieved from https://www.myhubintranet.com/collaborative-communication/

³⁴ Digital Workplace (2021), *op. cit.*

Batton, J., Jones, T. S., Cuervo, A., Bazron, B. J., & Gorin, D. (2006), *op. cit.*

³⁵ Digital Workplace (2021), *op. cit.*

Salem, R. (2003). Empathic listening. Retrieved from https://www.beyondintractability.org/essay/empathic_listening

³⁶ Digital Workplace (2021), *op. cit.*

³⁷ Batton, J., Jones, T. S., Cuervo, A., Bazron, B. J., & Gorin, D. (2006), *op. cit.*

Salem, R. (2003), *op. cit.*

³⁸ Officevibe Content Team (2021), *op. cit.*

³⁹ Dingwall, J. R., Labrie, C., McLennon, T., & Underwood, L. (2018). Conflict resolution. In *Professional Communications*. Ontario, CA: Olds College. Retrieved from https://ecampusontario.pressbooks.pub/profcommsontario/chapter/conflict-resolution/

⁴⁰ McShane, S. L. and Von Glinow, M. A. (2015). Conflict and negotiation in the workplace. In *Organizational behavior: Emerging knowledge, global reality, 7ᵗʰ edition*. New York: McGraw Hill Education.

⁴¹ Alper, S.; Tjosvold, D. & Law, K. S. (2000). Conflict management, efficacy, and performance in organizational teams. *Personnel Psychology*. 53(3).

⁴² Caskey, M. M. & Carpenter, J. (2014). Building teacher collaboration schoolwide. *Association for Middle Level Education (AMLE) Magazine*.

⁴³ McQuerrey, L. (2019). What are good people skills? Retrieved from https://smallbusiness.chron.com/good-people-skills-54765.html.

⁴⁴ Page, R. C. (2013). *Coaching winners! A Leader's toolkit for coaching & developing talent*. Minnetonka, MN: Assessment Associates International, LLC.

⁴⁵ Galinsky, A. D., Maddux, W. W., Gilin, D., & White, J. B. (2008). Why It pays to get inside the head of your opponent: The Differential effects of perspective taking and empathy in negotiations. *Psychological Science, 19*(4).

⁴⁶ Galinsky, A. D., Ku, G., & Wang, C. S. (2005). Perspective-taking and self-other overlap: Fostering social bonds and facilitating social coordination. *Group Processes & Intergroup Relations*, 8(2). https:// doi.org/10.1177/1368430205051060.

Wang, C. S., Kenneth, T., Ku, G., & Galinsky, A. D. (2014). Perspective-taking increases willingness to engage in intergroup contact. *PloS one, 9*(1), e85681. https://doi.org/10.1371/journal.pone.0085681

⁴⁷ Gehlbach, H. (2017). Learning to walk in another's shoes. *Kappan*, 98(6).

Krznaric, R. (2014). *Empathy: Why it matters and how to get it*. New York: Random House.

⁴⁸ Dikel, W. (2014). *The Teacher's guide to student mental health*. New York: W.W. Norton & Company.

⁴⁹ Bright Horizons Education Team (2021). Empathy: A Skill for future success. Retrieved from https://www.brighthorizons.com/family-resources/empathy-a-skill-for-future-success

⁵⁰ 4 Ways to encourage empathic collaboration (n.d.). Retrieved from https://www.ideou.com/blogs/inspiration/4-ways-to-encourage-empathic-collaboration

Chapter 6

¹ Finlay, L. (2008). Reflecting on 'reflective practice.' Practice-based professional learning Paper 52, The Open University.

² Parsons, M., & Stephenson, M. (2005). Developing reflective practice in student teachers: Collaboration and critical partnerships. *Teachers and Teaching: theory and practice*, 11(1).

³ Coffey, A. M. (2014). Using video to develop skills in reflection in teacher education students. *Australian Journal of Teacher Education, 39*(9). http://dx.doi.org/10.14221/ajte.2014v39n9.7.

⁴ Renard, L. (2019). How to become a reflective teacher – The Complete guide

for reflection in teaching. Retrieved from https://www.bookwidgets.com/blog/2019/02/how-to-become-a-reflective-teacher-the-complete-guide-for-reflection-in-teaching

[5] Pedro, J. (2006). Taking reflection into the real world of teaching. *Kappa Delta Pi Record*, 42(3). http://dx.doi.org/10.1080/00228958.2006.10516449

[6] Knight, S. (2018). Three reflective practices for effectiveness. ASCD. Retrieved from https://www.ascd.org/blogs/three-reflective-practices-for-effectiveness

[7] Collins, M. (2021). The Benefits of developing a reflective routine. Edutopia: George Lucas Foundation. Retrieved from https://www.edutopia.org/article/benefits-developing-reflective-routine

[8] Kamal, J. (2020). Making time for reflective practice. Edutopia: George Lucas Foundation. Retrieved from https://www.edutopia.org/article/making-time-reflective-practice

[9] Coffey, A. M. (2014), *op. cit.*

Spalding, A. (2020). How to encourage reflective teaching in your school. Retrieved from https://blog.irisconnect.com/uk/blog/5-benefits-of-encouraging-teacher-self-reflection

[10] Knight, S. (2018). Three reflective practices for effectiveness. ASCD. Retrieved from https://www.ascd.org/blogs/three-reflective-practices-for-effectiveness

[11] Kini, T. & Podolsky, A. (2016). *Does teaching experience increase teacher effectiveness? A Review of the Research* (research brief). Palo Alto, CA: Learning Policy Institute.

[12] Schwartz, S. (2022). How to give students the confidence to take on rigorous work. Education Week. Retrieved from https://www.edweek.org/teaching-learning/how-to-give-students-the-confidence-to-take-on-rigorous-work/2022/02

[13] Neer, M. (2016). How to learn better: Part 5 – Metacognitive. Retrieved from https://dataworks-ed.com/blog/2016/03/how-to-learn-better-part-5-metacognitive

[14] Teaching tip: Use metacognitive strategies to empower your students (2021). Retrieved from https://www.education.vic.gov.au/school/teachers/classrooms/Pages/ppn14metacognitiontip.aspx

[15] Renard, L. (2019), *op. cit.*

[16] Ferraro, J. M. (2000). Reflective practice and professional development. ERIC Digest. ERIC Clearinghouse on Teaching and Teacher Education, Washington, DC.

Marvel, A. (2018). The Place of reflection in PD. Edutopia: George Lucas Foundation. Retrieved from https://www.edutopia.org/article/place-reflection-pd

[17] Finlay, L. (2008), *op. cit.*

[18] Parsons, M. & Stephenson, M. (2005), *op. cit.*

[19] Toro, S. (2021). 4 Ways to get more from professional learning. Edutopia: George Lucas Foundation. Retrieved from https://www.edutopia.org/article/4-ways-get-more-professional-learning

Conclusion

[1] Gallup (2014). *State of America's Schools: The Path to Winning Again in Education.* Retrieved from https://carde.gsehd.gwu.edu/sites/ carde.gsehd.gwu.edu/files/downloads/reportGallupstateofschools.pdf

[2] Resiliency Initiatives (2011). *Embracing a Strengths-Based Perspective and Practice in Education.* Retrieved from http://www.mifras.org/know/wp-content/uploads/2017/01/Strengths-BasedSchoolCultureAndPractice.pdf

Lopez, S. J. (2011). Strengths-based education and student engagement. Gallup Student Poll and America's Promise Alliance. Retrieved from https://thecliftonfoundation.org/wp-content/uploads/2020/08/Strengths-and-Engagement-Findings-from-the-Gallup-Student-Poll.8706778a.pdf

www.ingramcontent.com/pod-product-compliance
Lightning Source LLC
Chambersburg PA
CBHW071854070526
44583CB00016B/1678